THE
KISS PRINCIPLE
Approaches to Building Reliable Systems

THE KISS PRINCIPLE

Approaches to
Building Reliable Systems

Ronald B. Smith

PBI

a petrocelli
book

new york / princeton

Designed by Diane L. Backes
Typesetting by Backes Graphics

Printed in U.S.A.
1 2 3 4 5 6 7 8 9 10

Library of Congress Cataloging in Publication Data

Smith, Ronald B.
    The KISS principle.

    "A Petrocelli book."
    Bibliography: p.
    Includes index.
    1. System design.   I. Title.
QA76.9.S88S65   1983   003   83-12087
ISBN 0-89433-198-1

*This book is in memory
of my father-in-law,*

Anthony Vastola,

*who died January 26, 1981,
from Multiple Sclerosis (MS).*

*Fifty percent of the royalties
from the sale of this book
will be donated to the research
of finding a cure for MS.*

"When you fail to plan, you are planning to fail."

Dr. Robert Schuller

"Common sense isn't common."

Will Rogers

Contents

PART TWO
Software and Hardware Approaches

Preface

The computer field abounds with controversy and different points of view. As Mark Twain said, "A man with a new idea is considered a crank until the idea succeeds." This book offers useful and practical ideas and approaches that have been tested on how to develop good application systems. For easy reading, the writing style here is composed of nontechnical language, graphics (approximately one-third of the book), and general narratives. The book is intended for data processing (DP) people (e.g., managers, systems analysts, programmers, and DP auditors), non-DP people (e.g., managers and executives), and could be used as a textbook at the college or university level for introduction to systems analysis or systems design. It is hoped the book will strip away much of the mystique of data processing and provide a better understanding of some of the approaches that can be used to build reliable systems.

The book has two related purposes. The first is to show how to build reliable systems by using automated methodologies. The second purpose is to look at alternatives to the traditional techniques of application development that can better serve and manage your organization.

Part I updates and defines the KISS Principle as it applies to data processing and describes the Systems Development Process (SDP). In conjunction with the SDP, automated development systems and structured design tools will be integrated together so that we can have reliable systems which are built on time and within budget and require less ongoing maintenance.

Part II deals with alternatives to conventional application development techniques which includes turnkey (hardware and software) systems that can be used as stand-alone systems, clustered systems, and/or plug-compatible with your mainframe computer. The turnkey systems include using a financial planning system, an automated records management system, programmable portable data terminals and the integrated electronic office. The last chapter is about our computer-based society and where it is going in the 1980s.

This book is not intended to advertise any particular hardware and/or software products; therefore, the vendor names have been changed for obvious reasons.

I do wish to thank the publisher, O.R. Petrocelli, and my wife Janet whose efforts, support, and understanding made this book possible.

PART ONE

The Systems Development Process

1

Introduction

KISS is an old data processing acronym that stands for "Keep It Simple Stupid." It is usually referred to in the building of new computer applications. The following is an expanded and updated definition of the elements that make up the KISS principle:

1. If you are fortunate to have a simple solution to a problem—keep it that way. Sometimes it is human nature to take a simple solution to a problem and complicate it. Quite often, today's complicated solution creates tomorrow's problems.

2. If the only solution to a problem is a complicated one, then the solution should be divided into simple and workable parts that interface with each other. The complicated solution should be like putting the pieces of a puzzle neatly together.

3. Once you have defined your solution, there will be many levels of approaches in planning, designing, and implementing your system. The difficult part

is to choose the overall approach and the many underlying approaches that are available. Because there are many time-saving approaches available today, the least desirable approach in designing a new system is to program it "entirely" in-house.

The following two case studies are experiences the author had that show common flaws in developing systems that you can run into by not adhering to the KISS principle. The rest of the book is about the different but sound approaches that can be used in building reliable systems and, at the same time, that help you to utilize the KISS principle.

CASE 1: FLAPS Flaws

The First Line Automobile Parts Company of Syracuse, New York, manufactured specialized auto parts for General Motors Corporation and American Motors Corporation, both of Detroit, Michigan.

The sales department had a manual system to compute and file sales quotes and margin markups for each part that the company produced. The company's sales had doubled over the last three years and were expected to double again over the next three years. The sales manager, realizing that it was getting next to impossible to handle this growing manual system, asked the manager of the company's systems department to design and implement a computerized system to replace the manual one.

The systems manager assigned the best systems analyst to plan, design, and help implement the system. The system was named after the company, First Line Automobile Parts System (FLAPS). The project, considered small in size and estimated to cost $14,000, was to be designed and implemented within 10 weeks. FLAPS required all input to the system to be generated via key-to-disk operations from the sales department. Computer processing would normally be on an overnight basis. The outputted reports would be delivered to the sales department on the following day.

The following are the three different key-to-disk operations:

1. *Maintaining the index file by index transactions.* The index transactions create and maintain the parts on the index file. The index file is an index of parts which may be obsolete, replaced, seldom ordered, or not found in the on-line parts master file. The only conversion requirement of this system is to take the card deck, which service parts personnel refer to as their "cookie jar," and convert this to the starting index file. The index file is one of the inputs into the next operation.

2. *Maintaining the quotes file by quote transactions.* The quote transactions create and maintain the quotes on the quotes file. The purpose of this operation is to provide part number validation, item pricing, and an 8½ x 11 quote (STD form) document suitable for mailing to customers. The effective days (life of quote) range will be from 1 to 120 days. Other than margin transactions, the quotes file is the only input into the next operation.

3. *Maintaining the quotes file by margin transactions.*
The margin transactions can maintain the quotes on
the quotes file. The purpose of this operation is to
give the sales department management the ability to
select various quotations from the quotes file and
analyze the margins by item and overall quotation.

See exhibits 1.1 and 1.2 for the pictorial requirements of
FLAPS.

Based on the scope and the requirements of FLAPS, the
systems analyst designed the system and reviewed it with the
sales manager. The review went smoothly, and the sales manager agreed with everything.

Then the systems analyst turned over the systems specifications to the programming manager. The design was
simple—three programs. The first program was to edit all
the input data, the second was to update the parts databases
with the valid input data, and the last program was to print
the reports. In short, the systems analyst was applying the
KISS principle in the design of the system.

However, the programming manager disagreed with the
design and decided to combine the edit and update programs
into one program and assigned the job to a junior programmer. After 13 weeks the programming was completed
and ready for testing. Every time the edit/update program
was tested it ABENDed. ABEND (abnormal end of task) is
the termination of a task prior to its completion because of
an error condition that cannot be resolved by recovery facilities while the task is being executed. The difficult thing
was to determine if the records were being lost during the

EXHIBIT 1.1 FLAPS flow chart of information flow

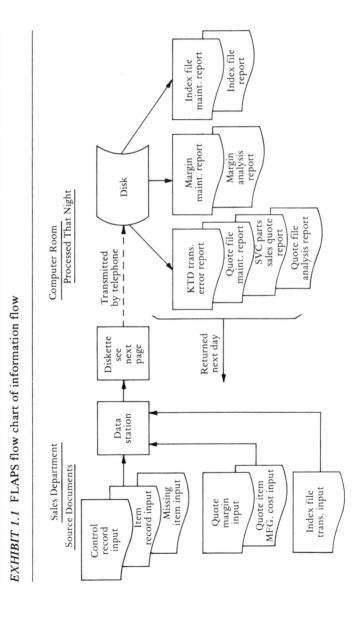

EXHIBIT 1.2 Overview of diskettes

The entire system consists of 14 diskettes. On a normal day, one diskette from groups 1, 2 and 3 will be submitted leaving 3 backups within each group. On the upper left-hand corner of each diskette is an external number label. The boxes below represent the diskettes with external number label detail and descriptions of contents:

GROUP 1

1. With exception of generation number, each diskette has same JCL.
2. Since there are 3 types of input transactions (1, 2 or 3), each diskette has same 3 programs for coding characters.
3. Always use the diskettes in descending order (generation no. 4 through 1).

GROUP 2

4. With exception of generation number, each diskette has same JCL.
5. Since there are 2 types of input transactions (4 or 5), each diskette has 2 programs for coding characters.
6. See number 3 above.

GROUP 3

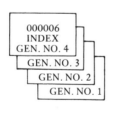

7. With exception of generation number, each diskette has same JCL.
8. Since there is one type of input transaction, each diskette has same program for coding characters.
9. See number 3 above.

editing and/or updating process. It soon became apparent that combining the simple programs (editing and updating) into one program resulted in one big complicated program. After another four weeks of continuous testing, all the wrinkles of the system appeared to be straightened out.

The analyst wrote the user procedures and turned them over to the users. Also, the users were trained to operate the data station. Finally, the system was implemented.

During the first month of operation, the junior programmer was called in on three different occasions (after midnight) because of an ABEND—records were still being lost within the edit/update program. After making programming corrections during the month, the system had no more ABENDS.

LESSONS LEARNED

Because of new programming techniques, there has been a trend toward cutting down the number of programs in a system by combining many functions into a single program. Recent experience shows that this is not always a valid assumption. In some systems combining numerous functions will work, while in others it will not work very efficiently. Each new system has to be looked at individually to find out if functions should be combined.

Exhibit 1.3 shows the analyst's systems design. The system should have cost $14,000 for 10 weeks of work with yearly production costs of $1,000. In addition, the system should have had a high program efficiency rating. Exhibit 1.4 gives the actual programming design. The system cost $25,000 for 17 weeks of work with yearly production costs of $1,500. In actuality, the system has a low program efficiency rating. By comparing the two figures, you can readily

EXHIBIT 1.3 Systems design

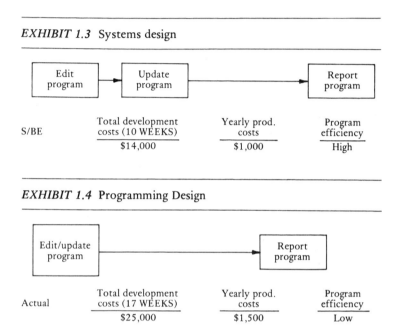

EXHIBIT 1.4 Programming Design

see the differences. The system cost the users an extra $11,000 to develop with an extra $500 for yearly production costs.

Table 1.1 shows the eight kinds of process combinations that can be found within any system. The chart rates the process combinations from the best situation to the worst. FLAPS falls toward the bottom of the range. The programming manager would have been better off giving the programming assignment to a more experienced programmer. Because of the lack of experience, it was not a healthy situation to put the junior programmer in. The junior programmer performed the best that he or she could do under the circumstances.

Table 1.1 Process Combinations

Total development costs		*Yearly production costs*	*Program efficiency*
Best	Low	Low	High
	Low	Low	Low
	Low	High	High
	Low	High	Low
	High	Low	High
	High	Low	Low
	High	High	High
Worst	High	High	Low

Sometimes it is human nature to take a simple solution to a problem and complicate it. Quite often, today's complicated solution creates tomorrow's problems. The lesson to be learned from FLAPS is that if you are fortunate to have a simple solution to a problem—keep it that way!

CASE 2: FLOPS Flops

Once there was a system to be designed call Field Labor Operational Payroll System (FLOPS). FLOPS started out as a good project, but ended up a dud and is still hobbling along. The purpose here is to show how things can go wrong on a project and the lessons learned from it.

There was a division which manufactured copying machines. As part of a conglomerate, the division's headquarters was located next to the conglomerate's headquarters. This division had branch offices in all of the major cities in North America. Each branch office had a terminal

NOTE: Case 2 is based on the article "FLOPS Flops... But Why?" by Ronald B. Smith. Reprinted by permission of *Data Management*, July 1979.

that was part of the conglomerate's communication network, which was hooked up to the main computer.

Each branch hired maintenance people from the local union to service the copying machines sold to customers. Each union had different pay rates and fringes for each job classification. The scope of FLOPS was to transmit the mechanics' weekly work data from the branch terminals through the conglomerate's communication network so that the mechanics could get paid. It was also to produce labor distribution reports.

PROJECT LOG

The following is the sequence of events during the systems development process:

January (first year).   The feasibility study began, and a user project manager, a user project leader, and two part-time analysts from DP were assigned to the project.

May.   The users approved the recommendations from the feasibility study, and systems design began. The cost of the entire project was projected at $50,000.

October.   The division elected a new president.

November.   The analysts gave a systems design presentation to the users. The president rejected it because the turnaround time of the communications network was too long. In a hold position, all work on the project ceased.

March (second year).   The systems design began again with a new cast, including a user project manager (president), a user project leader, and a full-time analyst from DP.

April.   DP upped the project price tag to $100,000 and a completion date of December. Also, DP decided (for the sake of saving time) to have programming concurrent with the systems design.

May–September.   The following events happened during the redesigning and programming phase:

The user project manager (president) was too busy with normal duties to be actively involved with the project.

In effect, the new user project leader was an interface between users at the local branches and the analyst. The user project leader spent more time designing the system than gathering the requirements. Also, the requirements were forever being changed. Many of the controls the analyst wanted were diluted or deleted by the user project leader.

For unknown reasons, the programming manager disliked the analyst. This created a difficult internal work environment for the analyst.

The scope of the project was being enlarged.

Because of the above events and the fact that the analyst was trying to meet the implementation date of December, the analyst's intrapersonal relations became unruly.

October. Systems design was completed on schedule.

November. Final programming estimates were made. For the second time the cost of the project was raised, from $100,000 to $250,000. Also, the implementation date moved from December to June. The users became very unhappy and, as an aftermath, the analyst was replaced with another analyst from DP.

February (third year). Testing of the system began, with many problems encountered.

July. Testing and parallel runs were completed and the system was implemented.

August–December. The following events took place:

The users were still modifying the system.

The internal auditors audited the system and were unhappy with the loose computer controls and the absence of noncomputer controls.

Top management wanted to know why the project was so costly, why it took 2½ years to implement the system, why the system was still being modified, and why overall controls left a lot to be desired.

LESSONS LEARNED

The scope of the above project had prearranged boundaries. If boundaries are continually being pushed back, then the chances of success are minimal. Also, the project should have had realistic implementation dates.

Users play key roles during the systems development process. To be effective, the user project manager has to have the time to be involved in the project. The user project leader cannot reverse roles, playing both the designer and the analyst gathering the user's requirements. As one can see, users can make the difference between having a good or a bad system implemented.

If the analyst who designs the system is working under a tight implementation schedule, it might be better if he or she were the test analyst because of familiarity with the system. Also, this could shorten the testing phase. In other instances, especially from an auditing standpoint, it would be more advantageous if the system designer and the test analyst were different people; for example, the user could be the test analyst.

The internal auditing department should be involved in all phases of the systems development process. This should help educate and impress upon users the importance of good controls.

A project will become unstable when there is a large turnover of users and analysts working on the system. The continuity, interaction, and transfer between the phases of a project will usually not be compatible and duplication of effort increases.

Concurrent programming with systems design on large projects has its benefits and drawbacks. The main benefit, if everything works, is saving of time. The main drawback is that the analyst changes specifications on something already programmed.

Due to changes in the business environment, there will be changes in the original requirements of the project. Due to changes in the technological environment, there will be changes on how the project will be designed, for example, IMS data bases and minicomputers. The longer the duration of a project, the more unknowns will be run into and costs will be correspondingly higher.

RECOMMENDATIONS AND CONCLUSIONS

DP should produce a systems development process (SDP) pamphlet for DP, management, and current and future project users. SDP is a structural approach to building information systems; it is simply a sequence of rational and logical thoughts and actions used regularly in making decisions. SDP is an essential tool that can increase individual contributions in project planning and development and can ensure project success. The aim is to educate the user in that role in SDP and as to decision points and risks.

DP should provide a standard control form to be signed by the user if he or she wants changes to requirements during the SDP. In this way, the user and DP will have documentation on one of the reasons why a project might go over its original cost.

Definition Phase

Initial investigation—identifies the problem or opportunity and determines the need for further study.

Preliminary systems study—provides an economic evaluation and first definition of the proposed system. The economic evaluation includes the "ball park" costs of designing and implementing the system along with the operational costs of the current and proposed system. The first definition describes all major features of the proposed system. The study includes scope, objectives, and constraints; identifies, evaluates, and recommends alternatives; and plans the next step.

Systems analysis—describes the proposed business system in user terms. It provides a business solution to satisfy the user's requirements and ensures that a technical solution can be developed and plans the next step.

Development Phase

System design—describes the proposed business system in technical terms that detail the logical system. It also develops plans for conversion design and user procedures. The conversion design builds a bridge from the current to the new system. The user procedures prepare the users to operate the new system. The next step is planned.

Programming—defines the programs and the modules within the programs, and translates each module definition into machine-executable code. Finally, the programs are tested both individually and as a complete system.

Implementing Phase

Testing and installation—tests all aspects of the business system to the satisfaction of user and data center in a "live" environment.

Project evaluation—reviews how well the system meets user business objectives and develops recommendations for upgrading SDP. This review should take place from one to six months after the system becomes operational.

ON BIG PROJECTS

All projects costing $25,000 or more should utilize PERT/CPM planning techniques starting with the preliminary systems study. On such projects, more work and the corresponding costs should be spent up front during the preliminary systems study. If not, the big project could exceed budget and implementation dates and be a poorly designed system.

Just as planning of a project is at two levels, so is budgeting. A firm budget is developed and a commitment made for the next step or phase. A "ball park" estimate is made for the total project. As the project proceeds, the estimate range narrows. Management is not asked to commit resources for the complete project until a clear picture of the solution is available. A complete solution might be obvious after the first step, or it may take a number of steps within SDP.

ON THE HUMAN SIDE

Since it is the user's system, the user must be made to realize that he or she has to have complete responsibility for controls. All too often the user does not know all the controls in a system and does not even realize the responsibility.

In FLOPS the analyst could not impress upon the user project leader the importance of good controls being built into and around the system. Therefore, the analyst should not try to mediate or correct the situation. In short, it could solve nothing and create ill feelings.

Most working people have one supervisor. An analyst has two, DP management and users. Since the analyst represents the users, it is his or her responsibility to let management know all possible consequences. If DP management decides to take no action about the situation, then there is nothing else the analyst can do. Therefore, the analyst must not be put in the position of trying to serve many.

FLOPS was missing one ingredient that brings stability to a project. It is called loyalty. For example, the programming manager put personal differences with the analyst ahead of the project. Also, the analyst was replaced after the final programming estimates were made. In short, the users held the analyst responsible for the increased costs and implementation dates. No gratitude was ever shown to the analyst for all the hard work put into the project.

No one person or event brought much harm to FLOPS. But, as you can see, the combination of people, time, and events can contribute to implementation of a poor system.

2
Systems Development Manual

This chapter concerns having a systems development manual in your organization. Since every organization is unique, this chapter is not meant to be used as a manual but rather as a possible outline for one. The systems development process is a structural approach to building information systems. SDP is simply a sequence of rational and logical thoughts and actions used regularly in making decisions. As such, it is an essential tool used to increase individual contributions in project planning and development and to ensure project success.

An automated project management system should parallel SDP. The automated project management system is used for planning, budgeting, and monitoring every work effort, thereby eliminating the negative effects of developing systems. This reporting system is described in the next chapter.

The rest of the chapter will be a pictorial walk-through of the systems development manual.

EXHIBIT 2.1 Systems Development Manual—shows the different
areas as a family that could use this manual

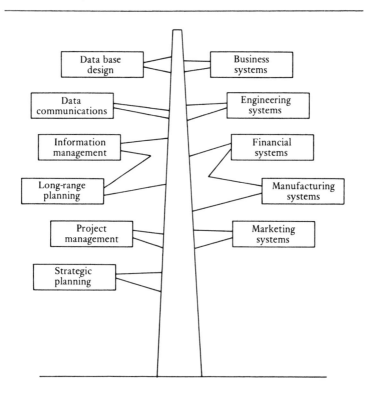

EXHIBIT 2.2 Risk/cost concept—shows the relationship of cumulative costs to the risks involved

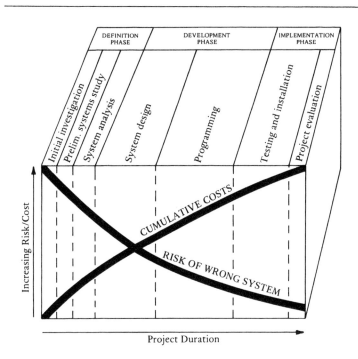

EXHIBIT 2.3 Gradual Management Steering Concept—shows the gradual commitment made by management for each step of the project

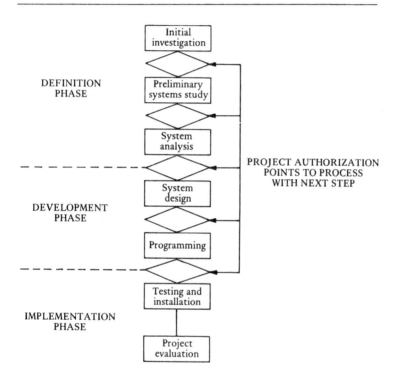

EXHIBIT 2.4 Systems Development Process (SDP)—shows how to walk through each step of the project from the bottom to the top step

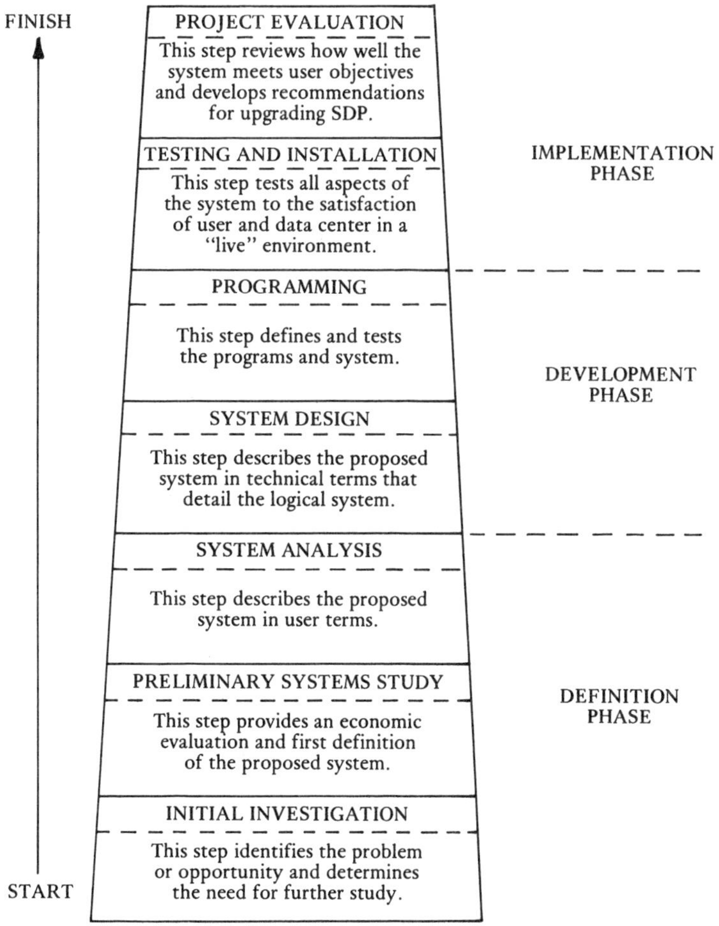

FINISH

PROJECT EVALUATION

This step reviews how well the system meets user objectives and develops recommendations for upgrading SDP.

TESTING AND INSTALLATION

This step tests all aspects of the system to the satisfaction of user and data center in a "live" environment.

IMPLEMENTATION PHASE

PROGRAMMING

This step defines and tests the programs and system.

DEVELOPMENT PHASE

SYSTEM DESIGN

This step describes the proposed system in technical terms that detail the logical system.

SYSTEM ANALYSIS

This step describes the proposed system in user terms.

PRELIMINARY SYSTEMS STUDY

This step provides an economic evaluation and first definition of the proposed system.

DEFINITION PHASE

INITIAL INVESTIGATION

This step identifies the problem or opportunity and determines the need for further study.

START

EXHIBIT 2.5 Logical Tasks for the Definition Phase—describes the
initial investigation, preliminary systems study, and system analysis
steps of the SDP

Step	Task Description
Initial Investigation	1. Project authorization.
	2. Resolve objectives and opportunities.
	3. Prepare report stating recommendations, alternatives, anticipated benefits and/or results.
	4. Prepare a preliminary systems study plan (schedule and costs) for the next step of the project.
	5. Present report and plan to users and management to secure approval for the next step.
Preliminary Systems Study	6. Collect and review present system documentation and current costs.
	7. Identify input and output requirements.
	8. Develop high-level systems flow.
	9. Identify in or out of house application packages.
	10. Estimate cost and pay back analysis.
	11. Prepare a system analysis plan for the next step of the project.
	12. Present plan to users and management to secure approval for the next step.
System Analysis	13. Perform data verification.
	14. Develop functional design, test, and conversion strategy.
	15. Review functional specifications with available application packages.
	16. Prepare a system design plan for the next step of the project.
	17. Present plan to users and management to secure approval for the next phase.

EXHIBIT 2.6 Logical Tasks for the Development Phase—describes the system design and programming steps of the SDP

Step	Task Description
System Design	18. Design and review data base.
	19. Identify test data requirements.
	20. Identify hardware requirements.
	21. Prepare detailed logical charts for each function.
	22. Finalize input and output requirements.
	23. Develop implementation/conversion plan and user procedures.
	24. Prepare a programming plan for the next step of the project.
	25. Present plan to users and management to secure approval for the next step.
Programming	26. Review systems specifications and determine program modules/job flow.
	27. Assign work to programmers.
	28. Review database design and program specifications.
	29. Prepare and walk through top-down diagram.
	30. Prepare test data.
	31. Code, debug and test programs.
	32. Prepare program documentation, operations documentations and production JCL (job control language).
	33. Test complete system.
	34. Secure approval from management for the next phase.

EXHIBIT 2.7 Logical Tasks for the Implementation Phase—describes
the testing/implementation and project evaluation steps of the SDP

Step	*Task Description*
Testing and Installation	35. Review conversion plan and systems test plan.
	36. Train users.
	37. Review user training manuals and computer operations documentation.
	38. Test complete system in a "live" environment.
	39. Verify results and conduct conversion.
	40. Obtain user acceptance.
Project Evaluation	41. Review how well the system meets user business objectives. This review should take place from one to six months after the system becomes operational.
	42. Develop recommendations for upgrading the systems development process.

EXHIBIT 2.8 General Roles/Responsibilities—describes the involvement of many categories of staff within the SDP

PHASE	STEP	USER		SYSTEMS AND SERVICES		STEERING COMMITTEE	EDP AUDIT	SYSTEMS REVIEW COMMITTEE
		MANAGEMENT	STAFF	MANAGEMENT	STAFF			
	Initial Investigation	AMR	P	R	CP	A	C	CR
DEFINITION	Preliminary Systems Study	RM	P	RM	P	A	C	CR
	System Analysis	RM	P	RM	P	A	C	CR
	System Design	RM	P	RM	P	A	C	CR
DEVELOP-MENT	Programming			RM	P	A	C	CR
IMPLEMEN-TATION	Testing and Installation	RM	P	RM	P	A	C	CR
	Project Evaluation	C	P	C	P	R	C	MR

LEGEND:
A = Authorize
C = Consult or provide assistance
M = Manage and control
P = Perform
R = Review or evaluate

Conclusions

Having and using a systems development manual in your organization will help you realize your objectives more effectively and sooner. The "successful" systems development process is the sum of the phased approach, management steering, and the automated project management system. The success of your system is the purpose and function of this manual and is a "smart start."

3

Automated Project Management Systems

The case of FLOPS Flops (chapter 1) was about a project that did not meet its implementation dates, went over budget, was still being modified after implementation, and was not a quality-built system. The story could have been rewritten as "FLOPS Tops" if the systems department had an automated project management system for planning, budgeting, and monitoring every work effort. An automated project management system should have the following attributes:

> On-line proprietary package for in-house installation. Package should be either easily installed and used or use the package on an outside time-sharing environment.

> Easy to learn, use, and requires no prior programming experience. Will use English-like commands.

> Provides training and implementation support.

31

Answers the crucial planning questions of what, who, how much and when.

Cost effective to use.

Reduces development and maintenance costs.

A good system for a development methodology which has a high degree of flexibility.

Handles a multiproject environment.

Summarizes project or projects.

Determines project trends.

Sets realistic work schedules.

"If what" planning and simulation capabilities.

"Done" and "to do" project steps and costs which reflect project history and future commitments.

Budgets dollars showing monthly expenditures and schedules expenditures based on the specific budgeting areas and their functions.

Need to manipulate large amounts of data and projects.

Retains data on accessible output files.

Easy input and fast changes.

Editing and refining capabilities.

Includes pictorial charts.

There are only a handful of software packages available that meet the above requirements. The two packages that we shall look at an overview of are JULIE and MICHAEL. These packages are cost effective to us and are proven products.

JULIE

JULIE is a computerized project management system. Exhibit 3.1 shows the overview of JULIE.

JULIE offers the following services:

Assign available people and machines to work on activities.

Determine when the project can be finished and at what cost.

Generate a variety of reports.

Produce quickly and accurately several alternative schedules which include CPM (critical path method) scheduling.

Schedule hundreds of activities according to their estimated duration and interdependencies.

JULIE offers the following reports:

Bar charts

Combined resource

Cost reports

Distribution of resources reports

Logic reports

Network diagrams

Tabular reports

Utilization of resources reports

EXHIBIT 3.1 General overview of JULIE

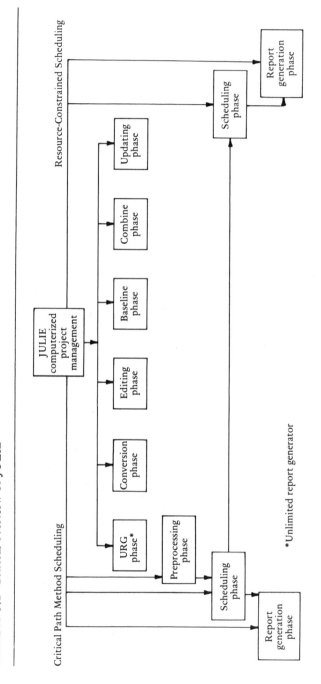

MICHAEL

MICHAEL is a project planning and control system. Exhibit 3.2 gives the overview of MICHAEL.
  MICHAEL offers the following services:

Automated network management

Automated project generation

Both process and event networking

Critical path management

Daily automatic load leveling

Extensive data validation

Reporting for matrix organization

Substantial audit capability

Total resource accounting and commitments

Unlimited "what if" simulation

Variable resource load smoothing

MICHAEL offers the following reports:

Accounting
  billing
  budget
Administration
  dictionary
  transactions

EXHIBIT 3.2 General overview of MICHAEL

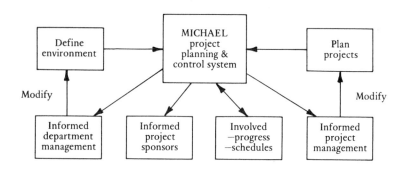

History and commitment of resources

category forecast by projects
category history by projects
project forecast by category
project history by category

Performance analysis

plan versus actual
prediction analysis
project evaluation
task evaluation

Project planning and control

bar charts
project analysis
project review by category
network analysis
trend analysis

Resource load and distribution

resource allocation
resource availability
work schedule

Conclusions

Project management can be broken down into two cycles—
planning and control. The planning cycle defines the project
goals and produces a detailed schedule on how they will be
achieved. Also, this cycle must be flexible enough to be re-
vised many times. The control cycle is an on-going process of
monitoring and updating that does not end until the project
is implemented.

An automated project management system should improve individual productivity and communications with the
user community. The system will define the roles and responsibilities of the EDP and user participants. Also, the system will meet time, cost, and objectives involved in the development of the project and at the same time maximize all
resources.

Not using an automated project management system in
today's large project environment is comparable to a man
who started his own business from nothing. Within the first
10 years, his business grew from 1 to 20 million dollars in
annual sales. Part of his success formula was to make all the
decisions and not to delegate any authority. Within the next
five years the annual sales increased to 100 million dollars.
In the sixteenth year the owner had a nervous breakdown

trying to run his company. The owner made the mistake of extending his proven control formula for a small company to a large company. Likewise, as the size of projects increases the ground rules must change to have a better control system. An automated project management system gives project managers a toolbox for a better control system. The most important aspect of using an automated management system is to eliminate the negative effects of developing projects.

4

Automated Design and Documentation Work Station

A company called Documaster, headquartered in Detroit, Michigan, markets a professional work station called the DOC 2000 that is used for automated design and documentation; see Exhibit 4.1. The DOC 2000 is a microcomputer-based data processing professional work station that allows an analyst/programmer to automate many of the tasks associated with the design, documentation, implementation, and maintenance of data processing software systems. It is a productivity tool that helps to solve the following data processing problems:

Limited data processing personnel resources

Increased volumes of user requests

High system maintenance costs

Inaccurate project costs

Inaccurate time estimates

EXHIBIT 4.1 DOC 2000 professional work station

Courtesy of NASTEC Corporation

Implementation deadlines

Requirement for high quality systems

Not having centralized applications design libraries to reduce duplication of effort

Managing the development process and responding to user requirements

Below are some of the salient features of the DOC 2000 professional work station:

Ergonomically designed and easy to use.

Real-time multitasking operating system and up to one million bytes of addressable memory.

Software for interactive creation and maintenance of graphics and word processing; see Exhibit 4.2.

102-key detached keyboard which includes single programmable function keys for the manipulation of commonly used design and documentation symbols.

High resolution display tube with 132 characters per line and 34 horizontal lines.

Vertical and horizontal scrolling.

Nesting—any block on the large overview flow chart can be assigned a file name. It is then possible to reference that file name and the system will seek out the more detailed and chained flow charts which expand upon that segment of the original overview chart.

Up to 120 million bytes of disk storage can be utilized.

EXHIBIT 4.2 **Text and graphics**

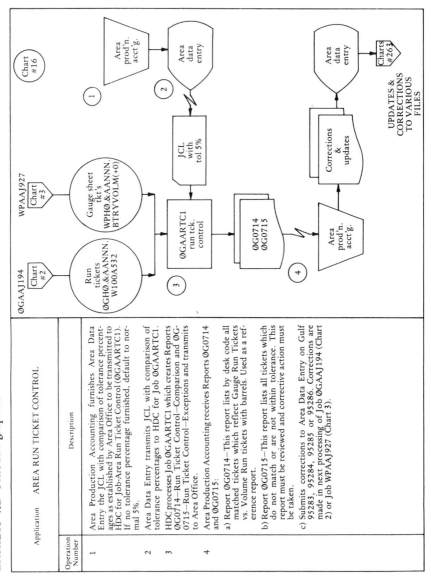

Operation Number	Description
1	Area Production Accounting furnishes Area Data Entry the JCL with comparison of tolerance percentages as established by Area Office to be transmitted to HDC for Job-Area Run Ticket Control (ØGAARTC1). If no tolerance percentage furnished, default to normal 5%.
2	Area Data Entry transmits JCL with comparison of tolerance percentages to HDC for Job ØGAARTC1.
3	HDC processes Job ØGAARTC1 which creates Reports ØG0714 and ØG0715: ØG0714—Run Ticket Control—Comparison and ØG0715—Run Ticket Control—Exceptions and transmits to Area Office.
4	Area Production Accounting receives Reports ØG0714 and ØG0715: a) Report ØG0714—This report lists by desk code all matched tickets which reflect Gauge Run Tickets vs. Volume Run tickets with barrels. Used as a reference report. b) Report ØG0715—This report lists all tickets which do not match or are not within tolerance. This report must be reviewed and corrective action must be taken. c) Submits corrections to Area Data Entry on Gulf 95283, 95284, 95285 or 95286. Corrections are made in next processing of Job ØGAAJ194 (Chart 2) or Job WPAAJ927 (Chart 3).

Application   AREA RUN TICKET CONTROL

Dot matrix printer (see Exhibit 4.3 for a listing) or a laser printer (see exhibits 4.4 and 4.5 for two different kinds of reports).

Up to 16 work stations can be clustered together.

Host communication links with IBM and plug-compatible mainframes (i.e., host disk dump for backup).

A small, lightweight data/graphics projection monitor can be interfaced with the work station to permit large group viewing in normal office lighting environments. This will allow one to walk through documentation in a review meeting, make changes immediately, get consensus on the spot, and at the same time maintain control of the meeting.

The following are some of the work documents that can be produced by the DOC 2000 in an actual work environment:

Change control documents

Change documentation

Computer room layouts

Data flow diagrams

Data segment layouts

Database hierarchy charts

Design flow charts

Forms design

HIPO charts

Organization charts

PERT charts

EXHIBIT 4.3 Partial Cobol Listing

```
00147  015900
00148  016000  01  FONT-NUMBERS.
00149  016100      05  MONTH-YR-FONT        PIC S9(4)  COMP  VALUE 0.
00150  016200      05  CAL-DAYS-FONT        PIC S9(4)  COMP  VALUE 1.
00151  016300      05  WEEK-DAY-FONT        PIC S9(4)  COMP  VALUE 2.
00152  016330      05  DOT-LINE-FONT        PIC S9(4)  COMP  VALUE 2.
00153  016400      05  JUL-DAYS-FONT        PIC S9(4)  COMP  VALUE 3.
00154  016500      05  DEFAULT-FONT         PIC S9(4)  COMP  VALUE 4.
00155  016700
00156  016800  01  DOTTED-LINE.
00157  016900      05  FILLER      PIC X(18)  VALUE ALL ".:.".
00158  017000
00159  017100  01  MONTH-FIELD-DATA.
00160  017200      05  CALENDAR-LOGO.
00161  017300          10  CALENDARLOGO     PIC X      VALUE SPACES.
00162  017400          10  CAL-CHARSET      PIC S9(4)  COMP.
00163  017500      05  CREATOR-NAME.
00164  017600          10  CREATORNAME      PIC X(30)  VALUE SPACES.
```

```
00165  017700      10  CREATOR-FONT       PIC S9(4) COMP.
00166  017800   05  CAL-HEADING.
00167  017900      10  CALHEADING         PIC X(52) VALUE SPACES.
00168  018000      10  HEADER-FONT        PIC S9(4) COMP.
00169  018100   05  CAL-NOTE.
00170  018200      10  CALNOTE            PIC X(52) VALUE SPACES.
00171  018300      10  CALNOTE-FONT       PIC S9(4) COMP.
00172  018400   05  SALES-NAME.
00173  018500      10  SALESNAME          PIC X(52) VALUE SPACES.
00174  018600      10  SALE-NAME-FONT     PIC S9(4) COMP.
00175  018700   05  SALES-ADDRESS.
00176  018800      10  SALESADDRESS       PIC X(52) VALUE SPACES.
00177  018900      10  SALES-ADDR-FONT    PIC S9(4) COMP.
00178  019000   05  SALES-CITY.
00179  019100      10  SALESCITY          PIC X(52) VALUE SPACES.
00180  019200      10  SALES-CITY-FONT    PIC S9(4) COMP.
00181  019300   05  SALES-INFO.
00182  019400      10  SALESINFO          PIC X(52) VALUE SPACES.
00183  019500      10  SALES-INFO-FONT    PIC S9(4) COMP.
```

EXHIBIT 4.4 Sales Orders Statistics Report

SALES REGION	LAST 3 MONTHS			THIS MONTH			FORECAST
	Actual	Target	%Tar	Actual	Target	%Tar	Next 3 Mtbs.
East	7.34	6.90	106	2.33	2.30	101	7.5
Midwest	3.65	3.95	92	1.15	1.15	100	3.6
South	2.66	2.70	99	0.95	0.90	106	3.0
West	6.05	5.40	112	1.87	1.85	101	5.7
Europe	9.12	8.90	102	3.10	3.05	102	9.3
Japan	2.28	2.55	89	0.83	0.85	98	2.7
South America	1.02	1.10	93	0.36	0.40	90	1.2
Canada	1.05	1.20	88	0.40	0.40	100	1.4
Total	33.17	32.70	101	10.99	10.90	101	34.4

EXHIBIT 4.5 Forward looking vintage chart

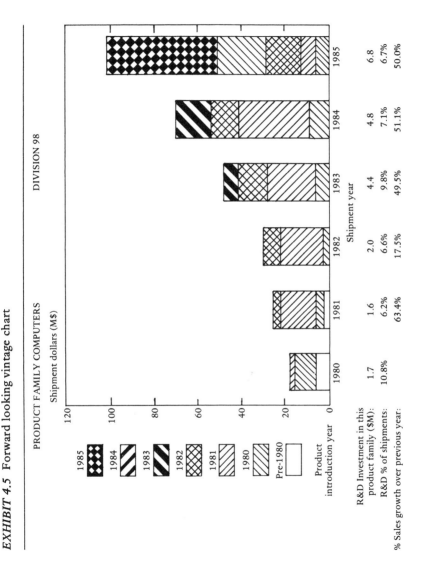

PRODUCT FAMILY COMPUTERS   DIVISION 98

Shipment dollars (M$)

	1980	1981	1982	1983	1984	1985
R&D Investment in this product family ($M):	1.7	1.6	2.0	4.4	4.8	6.8
R&D % of shipments:	10.8%	6.2%	6.6%	9.8%	7.1%	6.7%
% Sales growth over previous year:		63.4%	17.5%	49.5%	51.1%	50.0%

Shipment year

Product introduction year

1985
1984
1983
1982
1981
1980
Pre-1980

Production job books

Production control worksheets

Program narratives

Program structure charts

Project management schedules

Project plans

Report layouts

Screen layouts

Standards and procedures pages

System narratives

Work flow diagrams

In summary, the DOC 2000 has been developed to assist data processing organizations in meeting the expanding systems requirements of their companies. It provides a reliable vehicle for improving productivity by executing existing tasks more efficiently and introduces new policies and procedures into the development process.

5

Automated Software
Development Systems

Software development systems have been called source code
generators, application generators, and many other names.
They are a package of software tools to be used for the development and management of programs. Software development systems greatly increase the productivity of programmers by reducing much of the redundant programming efforts and generating error-free source code. This allows the
programmer to spend more time on complex tasks where his
or her skills and creativity can be put to better use. In most
cases, software development systems will handle 80-90% of
all programming requirements. The remaining 10-20% will
be covered by user code which can easily be entered into the
generated programs.

Most major hardware vendors sell software development
tools to run on their hardware. Many also sell software development tools to operate on some brand of hardware (i.e.,
IBM, UNIVAC, or DEC) and which generate some brand

of source code (i.e., COBOL, FORTRAN, PL/1, or APL). Since some software vendors live and die by the quality of their software development tools and not by selling hardware, more often than not, their software development tools will be better and more complete versus what the hardware vendors offer.

Case: TOOLKIT

A certain software vendor markets a software development system called TOOLKIT that runs on IBM mainframes and generates COBOL source code. Since most business applications are programmed in COBOL and most large companies use IBM hardware, this was an excellent market for the software vendor to aim its product to.

The TOOLKIT package includes the following modules:

System Information

  Menu system
  Documentation and help system
  Security system

Data Descriptions and Program Parameters

  File maintenance program generator system
  Data dictionary maintenance system
  Skeleton file maintenance system
  Libraries for commonly used COBOL routines
  Report program generator system
  Inquiry program generator system

Below are some of the benefits of using the TOOLKIT package:

Provides a complete standardized operating procedure which is a major quality/productivity improvement for the development of new systems and the maintenance of current systems.

Non-programmers can learn to make queries within hours, and users can write fully formatted reports after one day of training.

Can be used as a tutor to help train inexperienced programmers which will help to cut down on their learning-curve time.

Generates standardized COBOL source code from common skeleton files that is error-free and easy to modify.

Already existing compatible COBOL applications can easily be integrated.

Selector logic allows source code to be generated on one computer for another brand of computer.

Information is accessible from multiple data files.

Provides facilities for printing application/system documentation.

Can be used for utility "quick-and-dirty" and "one-time run" programs.

Allows management to allocate machine resources to the most important jobs running at any time.

Increases programmer productivity and contributes to a higher level of programmer satisfaction by reducing repetitive programming efforts.

Increased productivity will drastically cut down project times and costs by having error-free code, less time needed for programming, and a system that generates its own documentation.

The security system controls operator access to menu alternatives.

Yearly software updates, which includes expanding current functions and generating new functions per user requests.

A 24-hour dial-up "hotline" service.

Application Simulation Using TOOLKIT

Most users know their general requirements for an application but do not know the requirements in detail because they are dealing with an area in which they have limited experience. Users know generally what they want, but they cannot program something general—a program must be specific. The aftermath is a succession of post-implementation enhancements and improvements requested by users which greatly adds to the cost of the total system design effort. Application simulation is an excellent technique to close the communication gap between users and DP departments. TOOLKIT can be the means whereby users and data processing people work together to develop "quick and simple" throwaway programs that can be used to validate the concepts on which the final system will be based. The simulation adds a small cost to an organization's overall systems design investment, but will save money and time by preventing repeated system redesign which is a common occurrence. Application simulation will have a positive effect on organizational behavior in many areas (i.e., management of change and making the organization less complex) and will be a great joint learning system for users and DP personnel.

6

Structured
Design Tools

Structured design tools are documentation techniques and aids that help the systems analyst document the functional specifications of a system. The tools are graphical in nature, use plain common sense, and portray the system-to-be.

The author knows a large corporation that tried to introduce and standardize many documentation techniques at one time. It didn't work because it was confusing, and it is human nature not to accept a lot of changes all at once. The corporation should have selected and standardized a few documentation techniques that they thought would be best for designing new systems. As time goes on, new documentation techniques will be developed and the corporation should evaluate the new aids and decide if they will benefit the design of new systems. In summary, data processing departments should have a formal plan for adopting and implementing new techniques.

The following nine structured design tools are design techniques that the author has used at least once. Note that

there are many other design aids not portrayed and that new
ones are constantly being developed and should be evaluated
for possible usage. Also, the design aids can be used on the
automated design and documentation work station mentioned in chapter 4.

TOOL 1: Audit Controls

Accounting and data processing professions have related
that the documentation of controls for computer processing
is weak at best. Much personal experience agrees with that
premise.

LACK OF DOCUMENTATION

The use of computer-based business systems brings with
it special needs to establish and document controls over the
entire processing system. Many times there are adequate
controls in a system but the documentation is not standardized. The general purpose of controls in any system is to ensure that all data is accurately entered into the system, processed correctly, and the results verified.

The purpose of this tool is to illustrate a model for documenting controls for computer processing. This model can
be used by the systems designers, user department management, internal auditors, and independent auditors.

NOTE: Design tool 1 is based on the article "Model for Documenting
Controls Strengthens Weak Auditing Link" by Ronald B. Smith. Reprinted by
permission of Data Management, May 1977.

When writing the controls for this model, it is best to use as little "computerese" as possible. In this way, the nontechnical reader can better understand the control contents of the system. If the auditor wants more data, he or she can always go to the information processing department for backup details.

The following list reflects the eight standard control sections of this process model:

Control Section	Title
A	Controls Overview
B	General Narrative
C	Input Preparation
D	Input Transmission
E	Data Preparation
F	Computer Processing
G	Output Processing
H	Output Reconciliation

CASE IN POINT

Payment entry processing will be depicted in this model.

1. *Control Section A*—Controls Overview as indicated in Exhibit 6.1. The pictorial overview should come first because it is much easier to understand an illustration of the flow of processing than just reading words about it. For continuity in all overviews, it is best to use the same standard symbols. Always in-

---

EXHIBIT 6.1 Controls overview

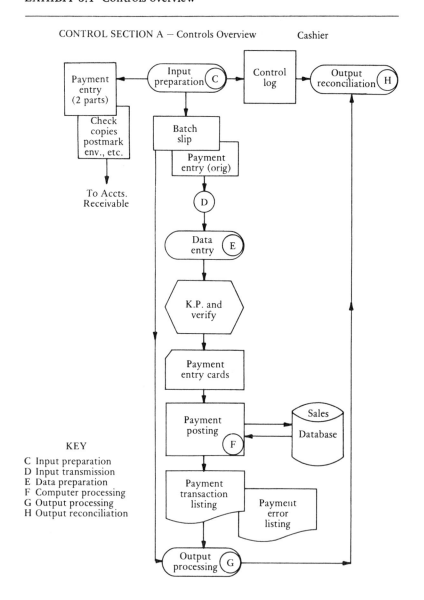

CONTROL SECTION A – Controls Overview   Cashier

KEY

C Input preparation
D Input transmission
E Data preparation
F Computer processing
G Output processing
H Output reconciliation

EXHIBIT 6.2 General Narrative

CONTROL SECTION B—General Narrative

Payment entry is the process by which payment for finished goods that are shipped and invoiced are registered on the database. This posting reduces the customer's total indebtedness figure and creates a payment record for use in later reconciliation to accounts receivable detail records.

It is essential that this function be performed rapidly and with extreme accuracy.

The methods used to control this processing are detailed in the other exhibits.

clude the user's title or user's department on the overview; this can be especially helpful to the user department management. The key (control section and title) is indicated in the overview for easy reference.

2. *Control Section B*—General Narrative as indicated in Exhibit 6.2. This is a brief description of what is taking place in payment entry processing. This should come immediately after the pictorial overview.

3. *Control Section C*—Input Preparation as indicated in Exhibit 6.3. From this control section on, parts of the pictorial overview are to be shown again, relating them to a corresponding control section. This saves time because it is not necessary to refer to the pictorial overview. The partial overview should be the same size and dimensions as it is depicted on the pictorial

---

EXHIBIT 6.3 Input preparation

CONTROL SECTION C — Input Preparation

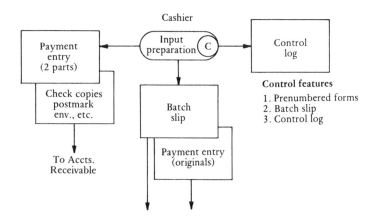

1. **Prenumbered forms:** The forms to which the payment data is posted are prenumbered and are used sequentially.
2. **Batch slip:** This form contains two controls in addition to batch no.: a count of the forms attached and the range of prenumbered forms numbers. The batch slip accompanies the input to data entry area where confirmation of the batch information takes place.
3. **Control log:** This log provides a place where the cashier summarizes and keeps track of all the payment entry transactions. Totals by bank by date are posted here. The date that each deposit was received from the bank, date sent to Data Entry, and date returned from Data Entry are also noted. When the payment entry processing by the computer has been accomplished, the totals by bank by date from the transaction listings are checked against the control log to ensure that all input has been correctly and completely processed. The log also provides a ready reference of batches in process, last batch number assigned, and a basis for analyzing the timeliness of paperflow.

overview. Also, each partial overview will be indexed by its control features. Below the partial overview, the applicable control features will be described. The input preparation controls are the prenumbered forms, batch slip, and control log.

4. *Control Section D*—Input Transmission as indicated in Exhibit 6.4. From this exhibit, you can see that there are no controls. This could be an indication there is a lack of and/or need for controls. If there is a need for controls, the situation should be investigated and, if possible, corrected.

5. *Control Section E*—Data Preparation as indicated in Exhibit 6.5. The data preparation controls are batch checking, key verification, and inclusion of batch number on each input record.

6. *Control Section F*—Computer Processing as indicated in Exhibit 6.6. The computer processing controls are input validity tests, error log output, transaction listing with control totals, and input-output total control.

7. *Control Section G*—Output Processing as indicated in Exhibit 6.7. The output processing controls are batch numbers on output.

8. *Control Section H*—Output Reconciliation as indicated in Exhibit 6.8. The output reconciliation controls are comparison of control log to output reports and comparison of returned input batches to control log.

A Standard Procedure and Standard Practice are referenced in this section. A procedure is a document that tells people how to proceed to do work. It tells a number of people or a number of groups how they fit into a single team play. The procedure instructions are written in a playscript format.

A practice is a singular version of a procedure that tells one person how to proceed to do work. Therefore, the playscript format is not used.

EXHIBIT 6.4 Input transmission

CONTROL SECTION D — Input Transmission

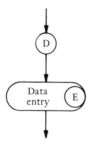

EXHIBIT 6.5 Data preparation

CONTROL SECTION E — Data Preparation

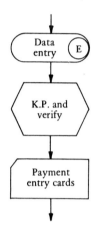

Control features
1. Batch checking
2. Key verification
3. Inclusion of batch number on each input record

1. **Batch checking**: Data Entry confirms number of forms on batch slips and range of prenumbered forms in batch. If batch slip isn't completely and correctly filled out, the cashier is contacted and the discrepancy is reconciled.

2. **Key verification**: The data from each P/E form is keypunched and key verified.

3. **Inclusion of batch number on each input record**: Batch number from batch slip is keyed into input record. The batch numbers then are carried through the program processing and appear on the transaction listings.

EXHIBIT 6.6 Computer processing

CONTROL SECTION F — Computer processing

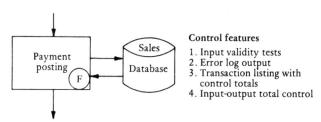

Control features
1. Input validity tests
2. Error log output
3. Transaction listing with control totals
4. Input-output total control

1. **Input validity tests:**
   a) On card code, source code, and bank code.
   b) Customer number tested by calc to Acct-Record in database.
   c) Payment reference number must not be on database—tested by calc to record in database.
   d) Deposit and remittance dates are checked for reasonableness.
   e) Payment amount must be numeric and positive.

2. **Error log output:**
   a) Complete input record shown.
   b) All fields which failed edit checks are indicated by an asterisk to right of field and headings name the field.

3. **Transaction listing with control totals:**
   a) All valid input is listed in detail.
   b) Totals are produced by bank by deposit date.
   c) Total net change to accounts receivable balance is printed at end of report.

4. **Input-output total control:** Within the program total, all input amounts are accumulated. At end of program, this total is compared to total net change to A/R balance. If they do not agree, a message is produced on the output report warning that an out-of-balance condition exists and instructing the cashier to notify the responsible analyst immediately.

EXHIBIT 6.7 Output processing

CONTROL SECTION G — Output Processing

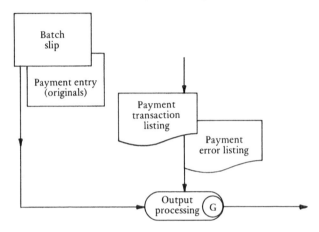

1. **Batch numbers on output:** The printing of batch numbers on the transaction listing ensures a positive link to the input documents. Input and output documents are matched up by data clerk and forwarded to cashier for reconciliation.

EXHIBIT 6.8 Output reconciliation

CONTROL SECTION H — Output Reconciliation

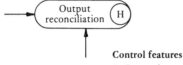

Control features
1. Comparison of control log to output reports
2. Comparison to returned input batches to
   control log

1. **Comparison of control log to output report:** The totals by bank by deposit date on the report are compared to the same totals which were developed manually by the cashier during input preparation. This procedure assures the cashier that all input was processed and returned.
2. **Comparison of returned input batches to control log:** This comparison assures the cashier that all input is being returned after processing. See Standard Procedure 10–1 and Standard Practice 9–3.

MOST IMPORTANT CONTROLS

The control features in this example cover a wide variety of techniques and methods. There are many other control features that were not mentioned because they were not applicable to this case study.

In some cases, a control section might be missing from control sections C through H because it is not needed or is not part of the particular processing. The two most important control sections are F, Computer Processing, and H, Output Reconciliation. These two sections should always be present and well-documented. Also, in some cases, a control section might be in a different sequence. For example, control section H, Output Reconciliation, might come before control section G, Output Processing.

The controls write-up can reference outside documentation. For example, Standard Procedure and Standard Practice were referenced in this case study.

Benefits of Controls

The user department management will take a more active part and interest in the system if it is involved in approving the controls of the system. Someday in the future that part of management's job requirements will be knowledge that the system has adequate controls or management will help implement the controls and responsibility for the controls. The user cannot always take for granted that the information processing department implements the proper controls for the system. Involvement is the key to educating the user and it also gives the user more confidence in the system.

The controls of the system should become part of the systems documentation book that the information processing department prepares for the user. Also, the information processing department should retain a copy for its own documentation.

Internal or external auditors always give high marks when they see this type of documentation on systems. The following are reasons why the controls write-up is a good reference for the future:

It is a reminder as to what the present controls are.

It can be used to train new employees.

Auditors who go directly to the user can see their copy.

Auditors who go directly to the information processing department can see their copy.

When modifying the system, the controls should be checked out for possible updating to make sure none of the controls were lost or to see if new ones were added.

If the present system is to be replaced with a new system, the present controls could be used as a guideline for setting up the new system.

From a systems point of view, writing up and getting management's approval of the controls has its benefits for the systems analyst. After approval, the systems analyst can write the specifications of the system for the programmer to code. Knowing exactly what the controls will be beforehand makes this job much faster and easier for the systems analyst.

CONCLUSIONS

The controls write-up, Standard Procedures, and Standard Practices should be part of the systems documentation book. Other sections within the user manual could include:

User manual distribution list

Application narrative

Flow chart of the information flow

Output descriptions with sample reports

Input forms

Definition of error correction procedures

Interfaces with other systems

Miscellaneous and correspondence

As you can see, there are many intangible benefits in having good documentation that are difficult to quantify in dollars and cents. One of the biggest areas of savings is in future time, and it's important to recognize that the cost of time in the future will be more expensive than now. The need for good documentation is becoming a very essential element for a good internal control system. This process model is offered as one vehicle for internal control since it is flexible enough to be modified to suit a company's own requirements.

TOOL 2: Relational Diagramming

Relational diagramming entails using symbols to present concise, yet meaningful, descriptions of a large amount of data (i.e., evaluations or broad comprehensive systems). The symbols represent components of the system, and it is left up to the user to determine the rules for using the symbols. For example, one could use squares and circles, and the different variations of squares and circles; see Exhibit 6.9.

CASE IN POINT

The author once had to review and rate many systems that could be purchased already programmed and used in-house for records management. The requirements (i.e., circulation and inventory) were similar to a library system. Top management wanted a final report, which meant a way was needed to summarize quickly all the data for the presentation. To avoid getting tied down in time-consuming detail, relational diagramming was used as the presentation format. Exhibit 6.10 shows the software/hardware rating review.

Letters A–E on the left side represent only row names, and column numbers represent the rating review from unsatisfactory to satisfactory. Tables 6.1A–6.1D are brief descriptions of the systems that got a rating of 1–8, with a more detailed description for the systems that got the highest ratings (9 and 10).

EXHIBIT 6.9 Relational symbols

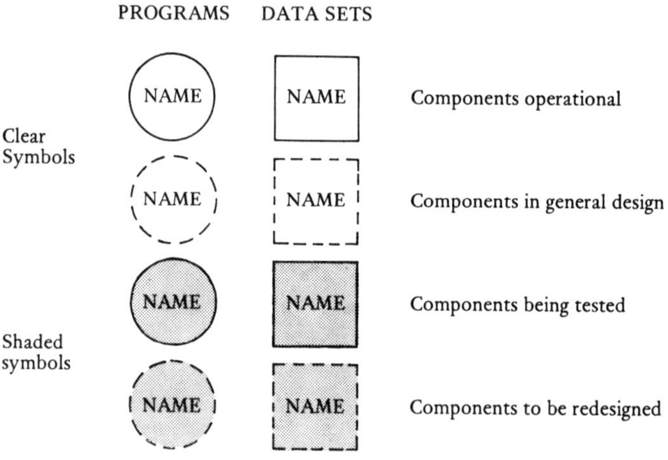

	PROGRAMS	DATA SETS	
Clear Symbols	NAME	NAME	Components operational
	NAME	NAME	Components in general design
Shaded symbols	NAME	NAME	Components being tested
	NAME	NAME	Components to be redesigned

EXHIBIT 6.10 Software/hardware rating review

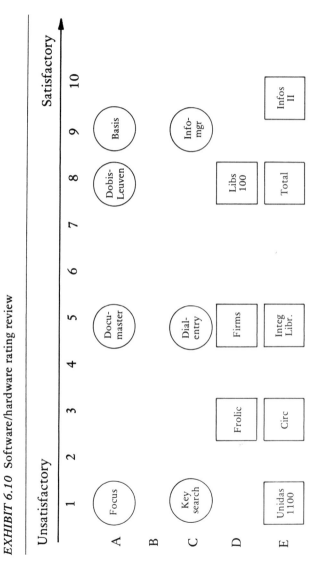

Circled symbols — Software package only
Squared symbols — Hardware/software package

TABLE 6.1A Rating List

Diagram Reference	Name	Supplier	Comments
1A	FOCUS	Vendor IB	No applicable library software and requires programming.
1C	KEYSEARCH	Vendor BI	No applicable library software.
1E	UNIDAS 1100	Vendor 1100	No applicable library software.
3D	FROLIC	Vendor D	Is a folder control system.
3E	CIRC	Vendor CLS	System is not large enough to meet requirements.
5A	DOCU/MASTER	Vendor TSIN	Does not contain library software for circulation and acquisition activities and has a limited number of reports.
5C	DIALENTRY	Vendor DIS	Is a private file service that uses an online data entry system for database creation and updates via Telenet and direct dial.

Diagram Reference	Name	Supplier	Comments
5D	FIRMS	Vendor GHT	System is not large enough to meet requirements.
5E	INTEGRATED LIB	Vendor EDS	System is not large enough to meet requirements.
8A	DOBIS/LEUVEN	Vendor MIB	Retrieval format does not allow for Boolean logic. Because the system was only recently introduced in the U.S., software updates, training, and support are questionable.
8D	LIBS 100	Vendor SYS	Excellent library system but not large enough to meet requirements.
8E	TOTAL	Vendor BAN	Vendor is just beginning to market TOTAL and has limited experience with it. Requires a programming staff to implement and support it successfully.

TABLE 6.1B Rating List

Diagram Reference 9A represents BASIS from Vendor BCL.

1. BASIS consists of a central system and modular components that can be attached individually or in groups. Included in the BASIS system is library management software that can be attached without any special programming required to support the library functions. Some of the modules that comprise the BASIS system are described briefly below:

   ● The central system can perform searches either through the use of an inverted index or through actual data records. It also affords the ability to perform proximity searches, to scan a database using prefix searches, and to perform hierarchical searches.

   ● The batch input module (or FORMS) option provides the off-line ability to create new documents, modify existing documents, or delete documents and to describe the data layouts.

   ● The On-Line Input, Verification and Editing (OLIVE) facility is used for on-line inputting and modifying of records in the database. It gives the user the ability to create, correct, and delete records; offers the flexibility to enter data in free-form or in response to automatic prompting; the capability to copy data from one record to another; and the ability to verify fields based on checks described in the database definition.

   Within one database, all the major functions of the library are automated: acquisitions, cataloging, circulation, and on-line services. The automated circulation function employs bar codes and light pens to activate the on-line editor (OLIVE), and the appropriate modifications are made to the circulation record in the database.

2. BASIS is available for a three-month trial period at a flat rate of $5,000. The purchase price of BASIS is approximately $100,000, which does not include hardware (e.g., more video-display terminals and hard disk storage). Also, the sheer magnitude of both the number of users and the volumes of records might dictate a dedicated host.

TABLE 6.1C Rating List

Diagram Reference 9C represents InfoManager from Vendor NDX.

1. *InfoManager* incorporates all of the capabilities of Creatabase and TextManager (see next two points) in a single system. InfoManager also has the ability to process structured data and unstructered text simultaneously from within the same database. InfoManager has Boolean logic and is operational on the IBM, Amdahl, CDC, and UNIVAC mainframes.

2. *Creatabase* offers capabilities permitting the rapid creation of a master file from one or more component files regardless of differences in structures. By reducing data to its absolute binary equivalent, Creatabase attains high-level compression, minimizes on-line storage, and operates at extremely fast speeds. Creatabase provides automatic consistency validation and builds its own data dictionary while creating a database. Creatabase offers a practical capability for database perusal or information browsing, since it features total access to the database regardless of its size or complexity.

3. *TextManager* is an associatively indexed storage and retrieval system. It offers a means of gaining rapid access to large bodies of textual material. The system is based on a group of compression and "mapping" algorithms; these permit the automated transformation of text to a fraction of its original volume. This transformation results in a unique representation which permits extremely fast searches of the database. Full text searches conducted on this condensed representation of the original files can be accomplished at extremely high rates of speed varying somewhat with the type of direct access storage units utilized.

4. The InfoManager prototype is available for a three-month trial period at a flat rate of $5,000. The purchase price is approximately $70,000 per mainframe installation. Maintenance will be provided after the first year at a rate of 10% of the purchased price. The purchase price does not include having more video-display terminals, hard disk storage, and the possibility of needing a dedicated host.

TABLE 6.1D Rating List

Diagram Reference 10E represents INFOS II from Vendor DATAGEN.

1. INFOS II is a database-oriented file management system that lets
users create, maintain, and use large databases in multiterminal or
batch environments. It is a superset of an ISAM file system. It includes a mechanism for data backup and recovery.

   INFOS II is a hierarchical system that offers multiple levels of index
files to access records in a database file. Keys in each level offer
fast access (e.g., customers by name and invoices by numbers); the
variety of possible index structures gives INFOS II its data access
versatility. By providing different paths to a single record, multiple
indexes eliminate the need for record duplication in the database.

   INFOS II has several features to manage file space efficiently. These
include space management, which takes best advantage of space
released by deletions, and key compression, which eliminates redundant characters by excluding duplicate portions of index keys.
These features can save a lot of disk space in a large multilevel
INFOS II system; they allow INFOS II to keep its files compact
and efficient without operator intervention.

2. *INFOS II Query and Report Writer*

   Query allows anyone at a terminal to examine index paths and database records, interactively. It contains extensive data selection capabilities based on Boolean and relational operators. Query can
also produce printed reports and summaries without an application
program. In short, Query is a user window to INFOS II.

3. *Recommendations*

   Have a six-month trial period (per vendor's new six-month rental
program) to implement and test lease records. The six-month rental
costs will be approximately $120,000, and most of the costs could
be applied toward the purchase of the system.

CONCLUSIONS

Relational diagramming has the following benefits:

Concise

Compact

Saves time

Shows system requirements

Aids in selecting priorities

Status reporting

Shows interrelationships between components
in a system

Graphic reference to the overall system

Simplified relational "snapshot" of the system

Can reference more detailed information

Focal point for a presentation

TOOL 3: HIPO

Hierarchy plus Input-Process-Output (HIPO) is a top-down graphical package developed by IBM. A HIPO package consists of a high-level visual table of contents and overview diagrams with low-level detail diagrams. Summation of the lower level relationships/functions equates to the higher level relationships/functions. HIPO's top-down approach results in a system of extreme modularity both in function and logical structure. The HIPO worksheet and the HIPO template are the two aids available for drawing HIPO diagrams; see exhibits 6.11 and 6.12, respectively.

EXHIBIT 6.11 HIPO worksheet

IBM HIPO WORKSHEET   GX20-1970-0 U/M 025*
                                                             Printed in U.S.A.

Author: _____ System/Program: _____ Date: _____ Page: __ of ___
Diagram ID: _____ Name: _____ Description: _____

Input	Process	Output

Extended Description

Notes		Ref.

Extended Description

Notes		Ref.

EXHIBIT 6.12 HIPO template

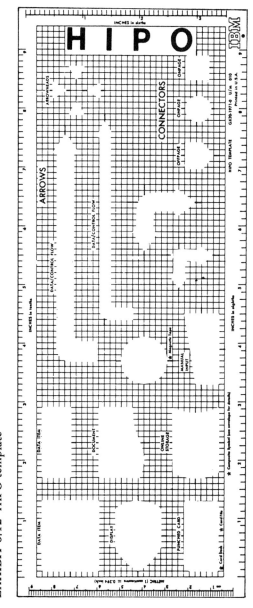

CASE IN POINT

The Area Data Entry Project was approved to replace the key-to-card system with a key-to-disk system at each area and to move as many edit checks as feasible from the host data center to the area offices. The new system will give much quicker response to error conditions. This will make it possible for the areas to correct errors prior to transmission and make the areas much less dependent on the host data center.

Exhibit 6.13 is the visual table of contents for the Area Data Entry Project. The high-level box 0.0 found at the top of the table is the name of the project. Boxes 1.0 (Create Host Programs) and 2.0 (Create Area Programs) are the two main functions of the system with more detailed functions found below it. The shaded box 0.0 corresponds to and is described on the modified HIPO worksheet in Exhibit 6.14.

One of the low-level boxes found at the bottom of the table is box 2.1.8 (Edit Reserve Transactions). See Exhibit 6.15 for the shaded box 2.1.8; its corresponding detailed HIPO worksheet is in Exhibit 6.16. (For more examples on HIPO, "HIPO - A Design Aid and Documentation Technique," IBM Publication GC 20-1851 is recommended.)

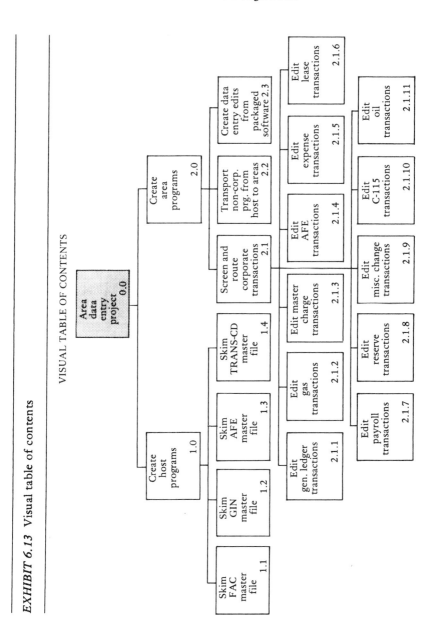

EXHIBIT 6.13 Visual table of contents

EXHIBIT 6.14 HIPO worksheet

Author: RON SMITH	System/Program: AREA DATA ENTRY PROJECT	Date: 11-1-82	Page 1 of 1
Diagram ID: 0.0	Name: AREA DATA ENTRY PROJECT	Description: AREA DATA ENTRY PROJECT	

Input

Output

Process

0.0 This project is divided into two top-level functions. The following describes these functions.

1.0 CREATE HOST PROGRAMS

Is broken down into 4 modules. The modules consist of skimming 4 different master files at the host to be transmitted to the areas to be used for batch edits.

2.0 CREATE AREA PROGRAMS

Is broken down into 3 main modules, they are:

a. Screen & route corporate transactions. This is further broken down into 11 edit modules which utilizes the master files created in the above function. After the transaction files have been edited and corrected, they will continue to be transmitted to the Host Data Center to go through the Data Edit and Collection System which is the current procedure.

b. Transport non-corporate programs from the host to the areas.

c. Create data entry edits from packaged software.

EXHIBIT 6.15 Visual table of contents

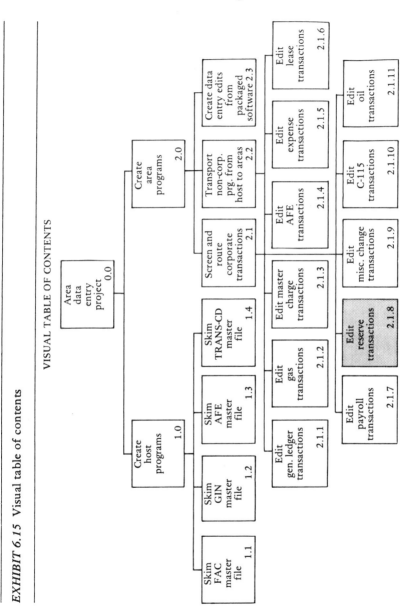

VISUAL TABLE OF CONTENTS

Area data entry project 0.0

Create host programs 1.0

Create area programs 2.0

Skim FAC master file 1.1

Skim GIN master file 1.2

Skim AFE master file 1.3

Skim TRANS-CD master file 1.4

Screen and route corporate transactions 2.1

Transport non-corp. prg. from host to areas 2.2

Create data entry edits from packaged software 2.3

Edit gen. ledger transactions 2.1.1

Edit gas transactions 2.1.2

Edit master charge transactions 2.1.3

Edit AFE transactions 2.1.4

Edit expense transactions 2.1.5

Edit lease transactions 2.1.6

Edit payroll transactions 2.1.7

Edit reserve transactions 2.1.8

Edit misc. change transactions 2.1.9

Edit C-115 transactions 2.1.10

Edit oil transactions 2.1.11

EXHIBIT 6.16 HIPO worksheet

| Author: RON SMITH | System/Program: AREA DATA ENTRY PROJECT | Date: 11-1-82 | Page 1 of 1 |
| Diagram ID: 2.1.8 | Name: CREATE AREA PROGRAMS | Description: EDIT RESERVE TRANSACTIONS | |

Input

- Reserve transaction work file
- Edit report message table
- Facility master file

Process

AS REQUIRED

1. Read in each record transaction work file.

   If record is a START or END record, print record on report.

   Otherwise, edit each record.

   If record passes all field edits, print record on report.

   If record fails one or more edits, go to edit report message table and get corresponding message(s). Print record and message(s) on report.

2. Make corrections on-line using original-input screen layouts and repeat process step 1.

3. The following pages define the:
   - record layouts
   - edits
   - master files used (if any)
   - edit report messages
   - report layout chart

Output

Transaction file

TOOL 4: Flow Charting

Flow charting is like using a road map to get from one point (start) to another point (end). As we are "walking" through the flow chart's logic, we will be performing many functions between the start and end points. Flow charting is a graphic representation of the flow of data through an organization and/or computer process. Two standard kinds of flow charting are used in data processing—system flow charting and program flow charting.

SYSTEM FLOW CHARTING

System flow charting is a general representation of the overall system that indicates interrelationships between the organization and/or computer process. See Exhibit 6.17 for the ANSI (American National Standards Institute) symbols that have been adopted internationally for system flow charting. Exhibit 6.18 shows an example of a system flow chart for processing payment entries within an organization.

PROGRAM FLOW CHARTING

Program flow charting is a pictorial representation of the machine functions within a computer program. See Exhibit 6.19 for the ANSI symbols for program flow charting. Exhibit 6.20 shows an example of a program flow chart for computing gross pay and includes a listing of the program code which was written in BASIC.

Program flow charting is an excellent tool for small programs. For large programs, it could turn into a monster for the creator. If a large program can be broken down into small manageable pieces, then program flow charting may be desirable. Remember the KISS Principle!

EXHIBIT 6.17 System flow chart symbols

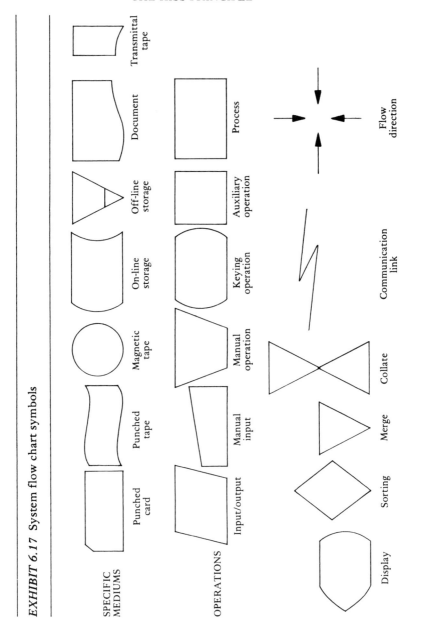

SPECIFIC MEDIUMS

Punched card   Punched tape   Magnetic tape   On-line storage   Off-line storage   Document   Transmittal tape

OPERATIONS

Input/output   Manual input   Manual operation   Keying operation   Auxiliary operation   Process

Display   Sorting   Merge   Collate   Communication link   Flow direction

EXHIBIT 6.18 System flow chart

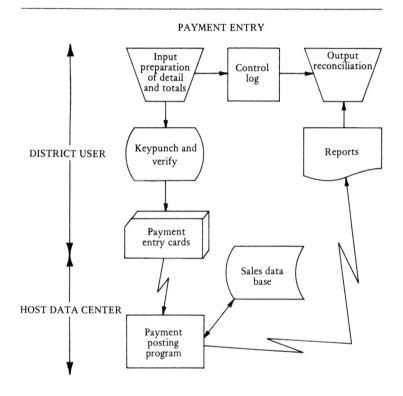

PAYMENT ENTRY

EXHIBIT 6.19 Program flow chart symbols

SYMBOL   REPRESENTS

PROCESS—a set of program instructions which perform a function.

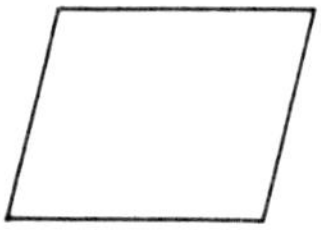

INPUT/OUTPUT—processing input information or recording output information.

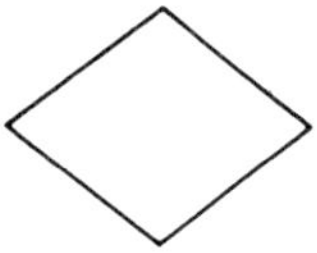

DECISION—a switching type operation where a branch to alternate paths is possible based upon variable conditions.

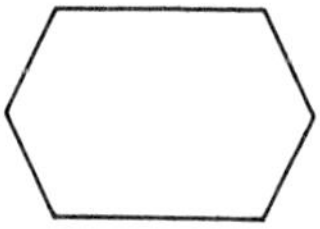

PREPARATION—instruction modification which changes the program.

PREDEFINED PROCESS—one or more subroutines not described in the particular set of flow charts.

TERMINAL INTERRUPT—start, stop, halt, and delay points within a program.

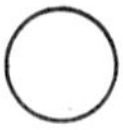

CONNECTOR—exit to or entry from another part of the flow chart.

OFFPAGE CONNECTOR—exit to, or entry from a flow chart page.

FLOW DIRECTION

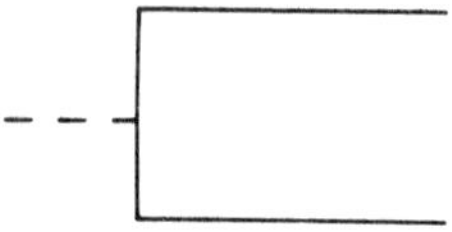

ANNOTATION, COMMENT

EXHIBIT 6.20 Program flow chart and the basic program

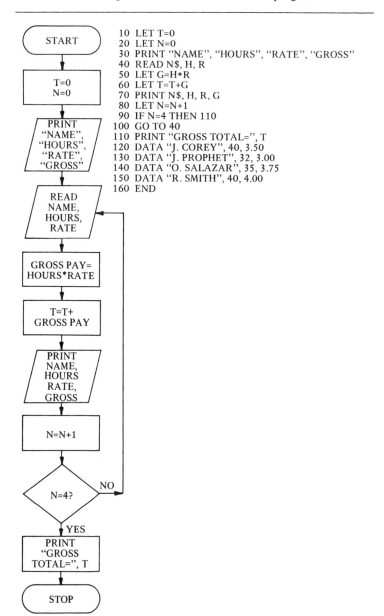

```
10 LET T=0
20 LET N=0
30 PRINT "NAME", "HOURS", "RATE", "GROSS"
40 READ N$, H, R
50 LET G=H*R
60 LET T=T+G
70 PRINT N$, H, R, G
80 LET N=N+1
90 IF N=4 THEN 110
100 GO TO 40
110 PRINT "GROSS TOTAL=", T
120 DATA "J. COREY", 40, 3.50
130 DATA "J. PROPHET", 32, 3.00
140 DATA "O. SALAZAR", 35, 3.75
150 DATA "R. SMITH", 40, 4.00
160 END
```

TOOL 5: Decision Logic Tables

A decision logic table is a documentation technique that can condense a lot of programming logic onto one page versus having many pages written to display all the elements of a problem. Also, it is easier for a programmer to code the "on" or "off" switches from the decision logic tables. The following describes the characteristics of a decision logic table:

Worksheet display of all elements of a problem.

Shows all the conditions affecting the solution of a problem.

Shows all the relationships that exist among the defined conditions.

Indicates which action or actions are appropriate for each set of circumstances of a problem.

Based on the *IF* (condition) and *THEN* (conclusion or action) concept.

Comprised of the following (see Exhibit 6.21):

Table header: name of the individual table.

Rule header: number of combinations of answers to conditions and their resulting actions.

Condition stub: a "yes" or "no" answer test to be made as part of the solution to a problem.

Condition entry: contains the "Y" (yes), "N" (no), and " " (blank) answers to the questions asked in the above condition stub. Blanks assume that the condition is not being tested.

EXHIBIT 6.21 Decision logic table

TABLE HEADER	← RULE HEADER →										
	1	2	3	4	5	6	7	8	9	10	11
CONDITION		C	O	N	D	I	T	I	O	N	
STUB				E	N	T	R	Y			
ACTION				A	C	T	I	O	N		
STUB				E	N	T	R	Y			

Action stub: itemizes all possible actions resulting from the conditions listed in the condition stub.

Action entry: contains the appropriate actions based on the various combinations of answers to the conditions contained in the condition stub. The "X" will indicate "take this action" and a blank will indicate "take no action".

SAMPLE SITUATION:
POPULATION CHARACTERISTICS

Problem 1—For each United States citizen we have a computer record that describes their individual characteristics. We want to know the totals for male and female Caucasians and male and female non-Caucasians. What will be the minimum amount of logic needed to code this program using the records as input? See Exhibit 6.22 for the answer.

Problem 2—Same as Problem 1, plus we want to know if the individual is under 65 years of age. See Exhibit 6.23 for the answer.

The following are the advantages of using decision logic tables:

Cuts down on the quantity of pages used versus using other forms of documentation.

Takes less time to program and debug from decision tables versus using other forms of documentation.

When used as documentation, are easier to change and update than other forms of documentation.

Can serve as check lists.

EXHIBIT 6.22 Race/sex table

	1	2	3	4	
Person Caucasian?	Y	Y	N	N	
Person male?	Y	N	Y	N	
Tally Caucasian males	X				
Tally Caucasian females		X			
Tally non-Caucasian males			X		
Tally non-Caucasian females				X	

EXHIBIT 6.23 Race/sex/age table

	1	2	3	4	5	6	7	8	
Person Caucasian?	Y	Y	Y	Y	N	N	N	N	
Person male?	Y	N	Y	N	Y	N	Y	N	
Person under 65?	Y	Y	N	N	Y	Y	N	N	
Tally Cauc. males under 65	X								
Tally Cauc. females under 65		X							
Tally Cauc. males 65 or older			X						
Tally Cauc. females 65 or older				X					
Tally non-Cauc. males under 65					X				
Tally non-Cauc. females under 65						X			
Tally non-Cauc. males 65 or older							X		
Tally non-Cauc. females 65 or older								X	

Should be used for complex problem documentation versus using other forms of documentation.

Saves time in defining the conditions of the problem, defining the actions to be taken, documentation, analysis, changes, programming, and training.

TOOL 6: Decision Logic Trees

Decision logic trees are very similiar to decision logic tables. The major difference is the format—a tree branch display versus a tubular display. Also, decision logic trees cannot condense a lot of programming logic onto one page like decision logic tables can. The following describes the characteristics of a decision logic tree:

Tree branch display of all elements of a problem.

Shows all conditions affecting the solution of a problem.

Shows all the relationships that exist among the defined conditions.

Indicates which actions are appropriate for each set of circumstances of a problem.

Based on the *IF* (condition) and *THEN* (conclusion or action) concept.

SAMPLE PROBLEMS

1. *Credit Orders*

A company that sells a product to its dealers uses the following criteria for shipping credit orders. If the order is for 12 units or less, and the credit department has approved the order and the quantity on hand is greater than or equal to the order size, the order is shipped. If the quantity on hand is not sufficient to fill such orders, it shows as a back order. If the order is for more than 12 units, the order is to be rejected. See Exhibit 6.24 for all of the possible outcomes.

2. *Simulated Craps*

We want to write a program to play craps. The usual rules for this dice game can be summarized as in Exhibit 6.25.

3. *Racquetball Tournament*

Ron (R) and John (J) are to play in a racquetball tournament. The first person to win 3 games wins the tournament. Exhibit 6.26 gives the various 20 ways the tournament can occur. There is a 10% chance the tournament will go to 3 games, a 30% chance it will go to 4 games, and a 60% chance it will go the distance, 5 games. The following are the possible outcomes:

RRR	RRJR	RRJJR
JJJ	RJRR	RRJJJ
	RJJJ	RJRJR
	JJRJ	RJRJJ
	JRJJ	RJJRJ
	JRRR	RJJRR
		JJRRJ
		JJRRR
		JRJRJ
		JRJRR
		JRRJR
		JRRJJ

EXHIBIT 6.24 Decision logic tree for credit orders

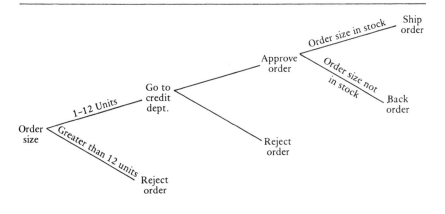

EXHIBIT 6.25 CRAPS decision logic tree

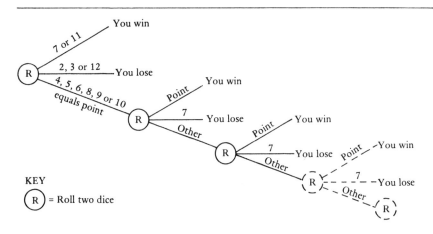

EXHIBIT 6.26 Racquetball tournament outcomes

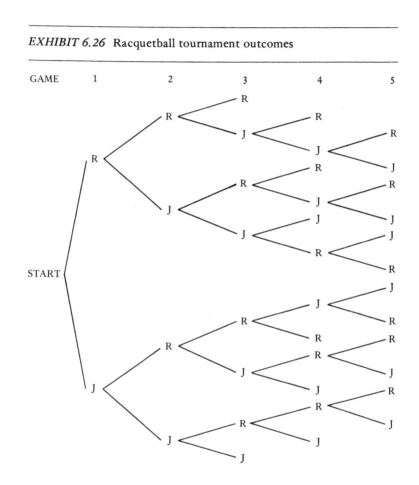

TOOL 7: Decision Logic Boxes

Decision logic boxes are a modified version of the Chapin chart which is very similiar to a charting technique developed by Nassi and Shneiderman. Decision logic boxes are a series of rectangular boxes and are very similiar to decision logic tables and decision logic trees. Below are the characteristics of a decision logic box:

1. Box display of all elements of a problem.

2. Shows all conditions affecting the solution of a problem.

3. Shows all the relationships that exist among the defined condition.

4. Indicates which action or actions are appropriate for each set of circumstances of a problem.

5. Based on the *IF* (condition) and *THEN* (conclusion or action) concept and normally displayed as YES or NO.

SAMPLE PROBLEMS

The first three problems are the same ones used in the previous section (Decision Logic Trees). They are used again here to show a different kind of display for the problems.

1. *Credit Orders*

See Exhibit 6.27 for all of the possible outcomes.

2. *Simulated Craps*

See Exhibit 6.28 for all of the possible outcomes.

3. *Racquetball Tournament*

See Exhibit 6.29 for all of the possible outcomes.

4. *File Requirements*

Define all the possible subroutines that can be used in calling in file(s) and define one of them. See Exhibit 6.30 for the results.

EXHIBIT 6.27 Decision logic box for credit orders

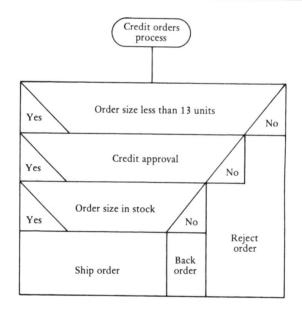

EXHIBIT 6.28 CRAPS decision logic box

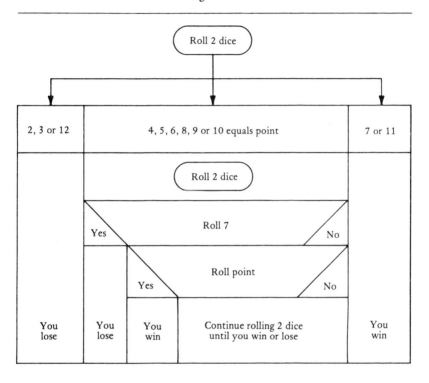

EXHIBIT 6.29 Racquetball tournament outcomes

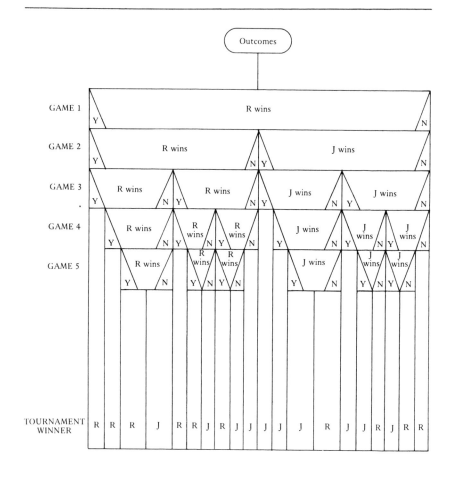

EXHIBIT 6.30 File requirements

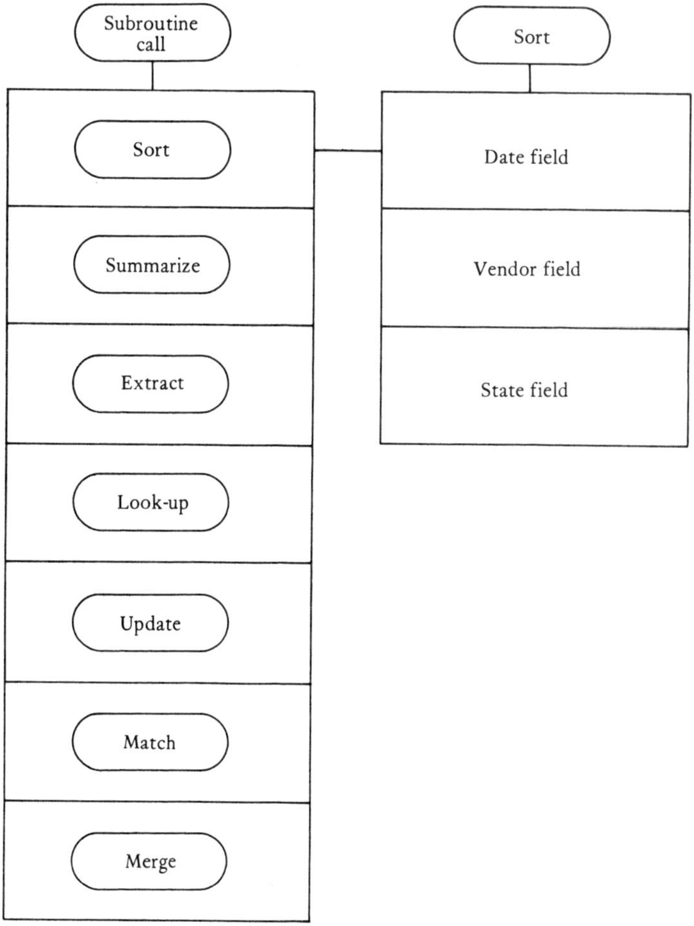

TOOL 8: Data Flow Diagrams

Structured analysis uses data flow diagrams as a starting point for writing program 'specifications for the system that is being developed. Analysis is the top-down design approach that depicts the logical inputs, transformations, and outputs. Data flow diagrams use circles as "process bubbles" and arrows to show data flows. The following are more attributes of a data flow diagram:

Paper prototype of the current and proposed system.

Pictorial network of the flow of data within the system.

Framework for doing the detailed specifications for programming.

Shows interfaces and interrelationships.

Shows components and their subcomponents.

Functional process that makes up the entire system.

Exhibit 6.31 shows the phases that make up the systems development process which includes the conversion design and user procedures.

Exhibit 6.32 is an example of a formal project structure. The phases are subdivided into activities, the acitvities are subdivided into tasks, and the tasks are subdivided into guidelines. The guidelines provide the "how to" and include extensive checklists, examples, and practical hints.

Exhibit 6.33 shows how to make a loaf of California walnut bread. The data flow diagram shows the ingredients, the measurements, and the various processes it takes to make the bread.

EXHIBIT 6.31 Systems development process

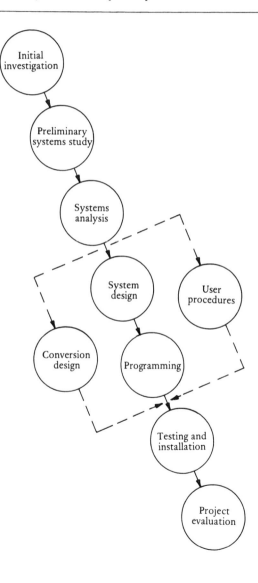

EXHIBIT 6.32 Formal project structure

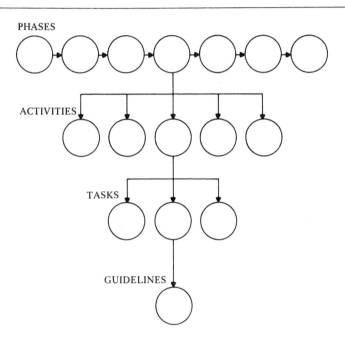

EXHIBIT 6.33 California walnut bread

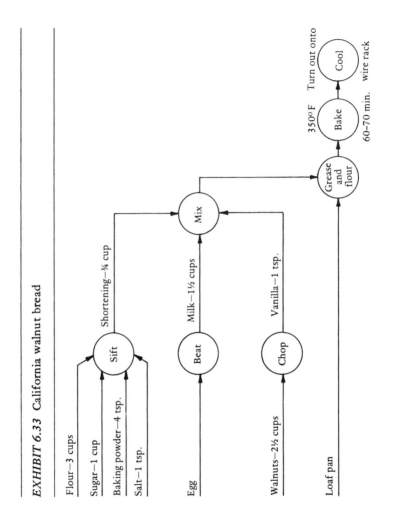

TOOL 9: Universal Record and Screen Layout

After using many different kinds of documentation formats for record and screen layouts, the author realized that it would be clearer and more productive to have a standard or universal format everyone could use and recognize. In that vein, here are two such formats.

UNIVERSAL RECORD LAYOUT

The following attributes describe the universal record layout:

Program
  name
Record types
  names
  number of records allowed per record type
  sequence of the different record types
Fields within record type

  short name
  common name
  place or field position
  field length or size
  usage or edits
  master files used (if any)
  edit report messages

EXHIBIT 6.34 One record type

PIPELINE AFE MASTER CHANGES

DETAIL RECORD (1 OR MORE)

SHORT NAME	COMMON NAME	PLACE	LEN GTH	USAGE	MASTER FILES	EDIT REPORT MESSAGES
********	*********	*****	***	*******************************	**********************	**********************
ZERO 1	ZERO FIELD 1	1	1	ZERO		E - ZERO FIELD 1
RCN	REPORT CONTROL NO	2-4	3	SEE CONTROL TABLE		E - REPORT CONTROL NO
DISTRICT	DISTRICT CODE	5-6	2	SEE CONTROL TABLE.		E - DISTRICT
DISTRICT				IF RCN = 155 157 205 242 277		
DISTRICT				397 OR 822, THE LAST DIGIT OF		
DISTRICT				DISTRICT MUST EQUAL 0. FOR		
DISTRICT				ALL TYPES (EXCEPT 7), THE 1ST		
DISTRICT				DIGIT OF THE DISTRICT MUST =		
DISTRICT				THE 1ST DIGIT OF THE AFE NO.		
DISTRICT				FOR TYPE = 7, THE 1ST DIGIT		
DISTRICT				OF THE DISTRICT MUST = 1.		
AFE NO	AFE NUMBER	7-11	5	NUMERIC. IF TYPE = 7 THEN		E - AFE NUMBER
AFE NO				AFE NO MUST = 0		
TYPE	CHANGE TYPE	12	1	MUST BE 1 2 3 4 5 OR 7		E - CHANGE TYPE
ZERO 2	ZERO FIELD 2	13	1	ZERO		E - ZERO FIELD 2
DATEMO	MONTH	14-15	2	NUMERIC. IF TYPE = 7 THEN		E - DATE
DATEMO				DATEMO MUST = 01.		
DATEYR	YEAR	16-17	2	NUMERIC		E - DATE
BUDGET	BUDGET CODE	18-22	5	NUMERIC. WHEN TYPE = 4 AND		E - BUDGET CODE
BUDGET				THIS FIELD = 0 AND BUD AMT		
BUDGET				GREATER THAT 0, THIS WILL		
BUDGET				CAUSE ERROR CONDITION.		
AMOUNT	AFE TOTAL AMOUNT	23-31	9	NUMERIC. WHEN TYPE = 4 COL 12		E - AFE TOTAL AMOUNT
AMOUNT				BUD AMOUNT (COL 32-40) CAN'T		
AMOUNT				BE GREATER THAN THIS FIELD.		
BUD AMT	BUDGET AMOUNT	32-40	9	NUMERIC		E - BUDGET AMOUNT
DESCR	DESCRIPTION	41-80	40	ALPHANUMERIC OR BLANKS		E - DESCRIPTION
********	*********			*******************************	**********************	**********************

EXHIBIT 6.35 Two record types

PROVED RESERVES MASTER CHANGES

DETAIL RECORD (1 OR MORE PER BATCH)
HASH TOTAL RECORD (1 PER BATCH)

SHORT NAME	COMMON NAME	PLACE	LEN GTH	USAGE	MASTER FILES	EDIT REPORT MESSAGES
RCN	REPORT CONTROL NO	1-3	3	MUST BE '151'		E - REPORT CONTROL NO
REC ID	RECORD ID	4-6	3	085		E - RECORD ID
CHG TYPE	CHANGE TYPE	7	1	1 2 3 OR 4		W - CHANGE TYPE
FAC	FACILITY	8-12	5	NUMERIC MUST BE > 5000. IF OVER 50000 MATCH ON FAC-MSTR.	FAC	W - FACILITY / E - FACILITY
FUNC	FUNCTION	13-15	3	NUMERIC		E - FUNCTION
TRAN	TRANSACTION	16-18	3	NUMERIC		E - TRANSACTION
JUL DATE	JULIAN DATE	19-24	6	NUMERIC JULIAN DATE		E - JULIAN DATE
DATACD 1	DATA CODE 1	25-26	2	NUMERIC		E - DATA CODE 1
DATAFLD 1	DATA FIELD 1	27-34	8	NUMERIC VARIABLE LENGTH. IF CORRESPONDING DATA CODE = 10 OR 11, TAKE FIRST 7 DIGITS OF THIS FIELD AND MATCH AGAINST FIRST 7 DIGITS OF GIN NO ON GIN-MSTR.	GIN	W - GIN / E - DATA FIELD 1
DATACD 2	DATA CODE 2	35-36	2	NUMERIC OPTIONAL		E - DATA CODE 2
DATAFLD 2	DATA FIELD 2	37-44	8	NUMERIC VARBLE LNGTH OPTIONAL SEE LOGIC FOR DATA FIELD 1.	GIN	W - GIN / E - DATA FIELD 2
DATACD 3	DATA CODE 3	45-46	2	NUMERIC OPTIONAL		E - DATA CODE 3
DATAFLD 3	DATA FIELD 3	47-54	8	NUMERIC VARBLE LNGTH OPTIONAL		E - DATA FIELD 3
DATACD 4	DATA CODE 4	55-56	2	NUMERIC OPTIONAL		E - DATA CODE 4
DATAFLD 4	DATA FIELD 4	57-64	8	NUMERIC VARBLE LNGTH OPTIONAL		E - DATA FIELD 4
DATACD 5	DATA CODE 5	65-66	2	NUMERIC OPTIONAL		E - DATA CODE 5
DATAFLD 5	DATA FIELD 5	67-74	8	NUMERIC VARBLE LNGTH OPTIONAL		E - DATA FIELD 5
-		75-78	4	BLANK		
DISTRICT	DISTRICT CODE	78-80	2	SEE CONTROL TABLE		E - DISTRICT
CTL DATA	CONTROL DATA	1-24	24	SAME AS PREVIOUS RECORD		E - CONTROL DATA
HASH ID	HASH ID	25-26	2	MUST BE '98'		E - HASH ID
HASH TOT	HASH TOTAL	27-36	10	NUMERIC		E - HASH TOTAL
-		37-78	42	BLANK		
DISTRICT	DISTRICT NO	79-80	2	SEE CONTROL TABLE		E - DISTRICT

See Exhibit 6.34 for an example of a program that only has one record type and does not use any master files for editing purposes.

Exhibit 6.35 is an example of a program that has more than one record type and uses master files for editing purposes. The example also shows the number of records allowed per record type and the sequence of the different record types.

UNIVERSAL SCREEN LAYOUT

The following describes data entry screens in general:

An unlimited number of customized data entry screens may be defined.

Records may be entered through single, multiple, or sequential screens.

Extensive data edit features are available to reduce errors in data entry:

format (alphanumeric, numeric, etc.)
size (maximum/minimum length, justification, etc.)
value (maximum/minimum range)
table checking
null value
interrecord field relationships
intrarecord field relationships

Can have full or partial auto-assignment of entry values.

Options are available for data edit and updates:

on-line entry and update
on-line edit and batch update
batch edit and update

Entry screens may be restricted by user ID.

Help text may be provided for each entry screen.

The universal screen layout should be composed of two major types for each set of screens per application. The first major type should be the data description index that gives the field length and usage characteristics and the screen character symbols used for the second major type—detailed screens.

See Exhibit 6.36 for the data description index. The top part displays the field length characteristics and the field usage characteristics (required edits, field types, and field programs). The left-hand side displays the number of screen lines that are available for usage. The bottom part displays the screen character symbols used.

Exhibit 6.37 is an example of a detailed screen or data entry screen. The exhibit shows the outline of a screen and its contents (field prompts and corresponding input fields). Above the screen outline, the data descriptions are defined (name, place, length, and usage) for the fields that are used within the screen outline. As one can see, it is nice to have a standard picture of a screen, its contents, and the data descriptions used on one form.

EXHIBIT 6.36 Data description index screen

```
                        DATA DESCRIPTION INDEX

       FIELD LENGTH CHARACTERISTICS ARE DENOTED AS INTERGER & DECIMAL PLACES
            EXAMPLES: 3.1 AS SNN.N = SIGN WITH 2 INTEGERS & 1 DECIMAL
                      2   AS  NN   = 2 INTEGERS
                      2.1 AS  NN.N = 2 INTEGERS & 1 DECIMAL
       FIELD USAGE CHARACTERISTICS ARE DENOTED BY SINGLE LETTER ABBREVIATIONS WITHIN
       PARENTHESES.
            ---REQUIRED EDITS---     ---FIELD TYPES---       ---FIELD PROGRAMS---
            (R)EQUIRED                (N)UMERIC              (I)SAM VERIFY
            (F)ILL-CONTROLLED         (D)ATE CHECK           (T)ABLE-LOOKUP
            (B)OTH (R & F)           S(H)IFT-INVERTED       R(A)NGE CHECK
            DI(S)PLAY ONLY                                   (P)ROGRAM GENERATED
            N(O)T REQUIRED                                   (Q)=(T & P)
                                                             (U)=(A & P)
     +-----------------------------------------------------------------------+
     | +                                                                  +  |
     | +-------------------------------------------------------------------+ |
  01 | |                                                   AREA - AANNN   | |
  02 | |                                                                  | |
  03 | |                                                                  | |
  04 | |                                                                  | |
  05 | |                                                                  | |
  06 | |                                                                  | |
  07 | |                                                                  | |
  08 | |                                                                  | |
  09 | |                                                                  | |
  10 | |                                                                  | |
  11 | |                                                                  | |
  12 | |                                                                  | |
  13 | |                                                                  | |
  14 | |   SSSSS    CCCCC   RRRRR   EEEEEE   EEEEEE   N    N    SSSSS      | |
  15 | |   S    S   C    C  R    R  E        E        NN   N    S    S     | |
  16 | |   S       C        R    R  E        E        N N  N    S          | |
  17 | |   SSSSS   C        RRRRR   EEEEEE   EEEEEE   N  N N    SSSSS      | |
  18 | |        S  C        R R     E        E        N   N N       S      | |
  19 | |   S    S  C    C   R    R  E        E        N    NN   S    S     | |
  20 | |   SSSSS    CCCCC   R     R EEEEEE   EEEEEE   N     N    SSSSS      | |
  21 | |                                                                  | |
  22 | |                                                                  | |
  23 | |                                                                  | |
  24 | |*************************************************************MORE*** | |
     | +-------------------------------------------------------------------+ |
     | +                                                                  +  |
     +-----------------------------------------------------------------------+



                             SCREEN CHARACTER SYMBOLS USED:
                                 P - PORT NUMBER
                                 S - SIGN OVERPUNCH
                                 X - ALPHANUMERIC DATA
                                 A - ALPHA DATA ONLY
                                 N - NUMERIC DATA ONLY
                             (****) - SYSTEM & ERROR MSGS.
```

EXHIBIT 6.37 Detailed screen

```
      SCREEN-40G                DATA DESCRIPTION
                       ----NAME----  PLACE  LNGTH  ------USAGE------
                       START         1-5     5     (S P) S='START'
                       JOB-1         7-8     2     (SNP) S='48'
                       JOB-2         9-11    3     (SNP) S='001'
                       POINT/ORIGIN  13-15   3     (SNP)
                       RCN           17-19   3     (SNP) S='151'
                       TRANS DATE    21-26   6     (SDP)
                       STATUS        28-32   5     (O Q) T='
                                                   OR 'FINAL'
                       AREA LOGON            5     (S P)
                       DATA FILE             8     (S P)

   +------------------------------------------------------------------+
  1 | +                                                              + |
    | +----------------------------------------------------------------+ |
 01 | |                                                                | |
 02 | |              VOLUME CONTROL SYSTEM              AREA - AANNN    | |
 03 | |                                                                | |
 04 | |                                         MONTH:NN YEAR:NN        | |
 05 | |                                                                | |
 06 | |START CARD:      JOB  P/O  RCN  TRANSMIT DATE  STATUS           | |
 07 | |          START  48NNN  NNN  151    HH/DD/YY    AAAAA           | |
 08 | |                                                                | |
 09 | |                                                                | |
 10 | |                                                                | |
 11 | |                                                                | |
 12 | |                                                                | |
 13 | |                                                                | |
 14 | |                                                                | |
 15 | |                                                                | |
 16 | |                                                                | |
 17 | |                                                                | |
 18 | |                                                                | |
 19 | |                                                                | |
 20 | |                                                                | |
 21 | |                                                                | |
 22 | |                                                                | |
 23 | |                                                                | |
 24 | |****************************************************************| |
    | +----------------------------------------------------------------+ |
    | +                                                              + |
   +------------------------------------------------------------------+

     OPTION:     NEXT SCREEN:    FUNCTION:
     OVERFLOW    SCREEN-40C      CHANGING 'START' CARD DATA


                              X - ALPHANUMERIC DATA
                              A - ALPHA DATA ONLY
                              N - NUMERIC DATA ONLY
                              (****) - SYSTEM & ERROR MSGS.
```

PART TWO

Software
and
Hardware
Approaches

7

The
Pollution Solution

A large diversified company in Canada that manufactures refrigeration units and related products is composed of 20 divisions that specialize in certain marketing areas. One of the divisions is called COLDQUEEN. COLDQUEEN came into being in 1970 and comprises four reporting groups: engineering, manufacturing, service parts, and accounting. This story is about the archaic service parts system, its problems, and a possible solution.

History

The following is the history of the service parts system.

1970

The manual system consisted of shippers, invoices, and balance-on-hand cards. The balance-on-hand cards were continually maintained for additions and deletions. The product

117

lines were truck/trailer, bus/rail, container, marine, military, and aircraft. The truck/trailer, bus/rail, container, and aircraft parts were handled by separate individuals. The marine and military parts were handled by one person because it was a manual job-cost system.

1971

The manual system was broken down into functional work groups: order handling, material control, and customer service; each group was headed by a supervisor. The six different product lines were lumped together for inventories, ordering, and typing shippers and invoices. In summary, the people were cross-trained for all of the product lines.

1973

The service parts group realized it needed a mechanized system to replace the manual system. The corporate system's department suggested it copy the service parts computer system that a larger division was using. Therefore, COLDQUEEN copied and implemented most of the service programs from the larger division for a cost of $20,000.

The following were the key reports from the batch system.

Adjustments (back orders, customer address, invoices, part number chains)

Back order status

Customer master records

Gross margin analysis

Invoices
Location of part numbers in warehouse
Open shippers created and not billed
Sales orders
Service parts year-end inventory
Stock status

1974

Service parts spent $12,000 to add a few programs and for maintenance of the system.

1975

Service parts spent $14,000 to add a few programs and for maintenance of the system.

1976

Service parts spent $16,000 to add a few programs and for maintenance of the system.

1977

Service parts spent $18,000 to add a few programs and for maintenance of the system.

1978

Service parts spent $20,000 to add a few programs and for maintenance of the system.

1979

Service parts spent $20,000 for maintenance of the system.

The above excludes the cost of running the system. So far, the service parts group has spent $120,000 for the system, and this amount will grow every year. Spending more money on this system is a complete waste.

Conclusions

In 1973, the system that was copied was 15 years old, had gone through three different hardware conversions, and was saturated with maintenance changes. Also, the system was designed with a lack of programming standards. Therefore, this was a polluted and outdated system that COLDQUEEN was buying into.

The system did, however, have some benefits:

Eliminated two typists.

Produced and shipped within 24 hours of order.

Generated back order shippers within 24 hours after material became available in inventory.

Faster invoicing.

More control over shipping/billing functions.

Short-term problems associated with the system were no user training, learning curve, unfamiliarity with output, and growing pains.

Long-term problems with the system were extensive. First, one mistake in entering data into the system had a ripple effect in the system by causing six or seven mistakes. To correct all the mistakes is a very time-consuming venture which service parts people do not have the time to do. Some of the mistakes cannot be corrected or explained. This is called the full moon, raining and midnight in China syndrome.

Second, sometimes the service parts people had to substitute a manual transaction to correct an error by inputting a transaction into the system to force the system to have the right outcome. For example, service parts received an incorrect invoice and its total card. Service parts destroyed the two outputs, typed an invoice, and keypunched a new card. To circumvent the system, the new total card was inputted into the total transaction program. Therefore, there was too much manual intervention in the system.

Third, part card system.

Fourth, insufficient controls to monitor the total system.

Fifth, no documentation of system and no user training procedures for new employees.

Sixth, lost output from the computer center caused by poor controls by the output section of operations.

Seventh, since the system was in batch mode, long delays were common between data preparation and the outputted reports. For example, the inventory reports might become out of date before they were finished printing.

Eighth, communications with operations were poor because of the following:

Service parts people worked the first shift.

Operations ran the system on the third shift.

Operations had a high turnover of people.
Service parts people were not always talking to the operational people doing the work. Therefore, no working relations were built with operations.

The more people involved caused more talking, less productive work, and more chances for mistakes and/or misunderstandings.

When problems came up, no one knew who had the responsibility (user, operation, programming) to correct the situation. This often caused friction between groups and magnified problems. The system needed an ombudsman.

For all the money COLDQUEEN spent, they could have bought an on-line order entry and inventory control package with the following features:

1. On-line transaction processing and interactive inquiry to facilitate more accurate business decisions based on timely information.

2. Video-display terminals to maintain a file of customer names, service part descriptions, and both open and shipped orders.

3. Display of the status, location, and inventory of every part. As orders are entered, shipped, or back ordered, inventory levels are updated immediately.

4. On-line editing to eliminate batch edit/error reports.

5. Override ability for all data items.

6. On-line functions which include the following:

Order entry
Order maintenance
Order retrieval by open orders, hold orders, or
  customer
Customer master file maintenance
Invoicing
Stock status
Transaction register

7. The batch part of the system which includes the following:

Inventory
Backlog
Standard cost
Gross margin analysis
Audit trail
Back order list
Shipper and invoice documents
Daily sales transaction analysis
Daily shipment analysis

Some of the advantages of this package are listed below:

1. Job enrichment.

2. System can be learned quickly and new operators trained easily.

3. Documentation.

4. Implementation and technical support from the company that supplied the software package.

5. Built-in controls.

6. Extensive editing.

7. Override ability.

8. Input batch balancing.

9. Little or no money spent on the maintenance of the system.

10. Since all customer-related data is available through on-line retrieval, customer inquiries can be answered immediately, thereby improving customer relations.

When a company needs a system, one of the first tasks should be software analysis and application analysis. This analysis should include reviewing computer program packages already in-house to determine if they can be used. If not, software packages sold by outside vendors should be evaluated for possible use. Going to an outside vendor can save a company much time and money.

8

Insight into a
Financial Planning System

Let us look at some possible alternatives to the traditional data processing life cycle for business applications. This chapter and the next will look at two different approaches.

There are dozens of financial modeling languages in use today, but relatively few are available as proprietary packages for in-house installation. The proprietary package that we shall look at here is called INSIGHT.

INSIGHT is a modeling and reporting system that can be used easily by accountants, business managers, and other non-DP personnel to generate financial and management reports. The language that runs INSIGHT is a transparent computer language that is easy for a non-programmer to learn and use, and this tool is becoming increasingly flexible. The most common usage of INSIGHT is in a time-sharing environment which is access to the computer from typewriter-like terminals (video-display screens and/or keyboard printer terminals) over phone lines.

There are a number of advantages of using INSIGHT.
First, the traditional business application can take six or
more months to implement: the user works through the systems analyst; the systems analyst works through the programmer; the programmer works through computer operations. As you can see, this can be a very time-consuming and
expensive business application for the user. Quite often, after
the application is implemented, the user is not happy with
the outputs and the above working cycle starts over for the
modification. With INSIGHT, however, the user circumvents
the user-system's analyst-programmer-computer operations
cycle by setting up his or her own application. The major
investment of the user using INSIGHT is his or her own time.
It takes only minutes or a few hours to design and implement a business application. The main difference between
an INSIGHT model and the traditional program is that the
model combines the input process, while the program has a
separate input and process. See Exhibit 8.1.

Second, INSIGHT is easy to learn and use by using only
English instructions.

Third, computer-printed reports that would take days
or weeks to produce manually can be generated in a matter
of minutes.

Fourth, the user's attention is focused on reports and
not on the computer.

Fifth, INSIGHT has a database for storing and retrieving
a number of business applications (models).

Sixth, INSIGHT has the ability to change the reporting
logic quickly (calculations, relationships, and report formats).

EXHIBIT 8.1

INSIGHT MODEL   TRADITIONAL PROGRAM

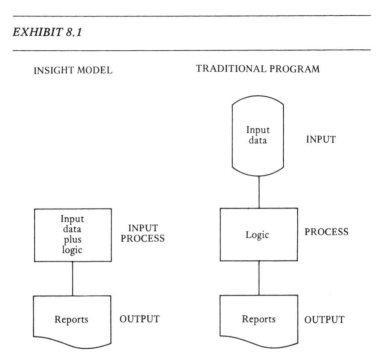

Among the features of INSIGHT are the following:

1. Financial planning, forecasting, analysis, modeling, and "what if" simulation to explore alternative solutions.
2. Automated financial routines—amortize, annuity, depreciate, discount, present value, rate of return, and spread.
3. Consolidation of models—consolmerge and consolselect.
4. Sophisticated reporting—report generator/writer with variable page length and width.
5. Plotting line or bar graphs.

Before relating a specific business application, let us define a few INSIGHT terms:

Model—a user-defined business application which consists of a matrix in which the user defines the logic. The matrix is made up of lines and columns and their interrelationships. The model contains column headings, line numbers with names, and definitions of reports to be printed. Each model can have up to 10 different reports.

Disk files—a file that permanently stores repetitive commands instead of wasting time entering each individual command. This means there will be less potential to make errors. The command to execute the disk file is INPUT DISK NAME-OF-FILE.

Report generator—the standard report format found within a model may need some fine tuning or window dressing. Using this feature, the user creates a file containing the report editing and formatting instructions. The command to execute the report generator after the model is called into memory is:

WRITER

NAME-OF-FILE

Case in Point

The consolidation of branch profit and loss statements for the Smith Transport Company will be used as an example. The systems overview is broken down into four areas: input models, disk files, output models, and output reports. See Exhibit 8.2.

INPUT MODELS

The five branches owned and operated by the Smith Transport Company are located in Los Angeles, Chicago, Council Bluffs, Charlotte, and Syracuse. The following are the names of the input models:

Actual	Budget	Prior Year
ACT-LOSA	BUD-LOSA	PRI-LOSA
ACT-CHIC	BUD-CHIC	PRI-CHIC
ACT-COUN	BUD-COUN	PRI-COUN
ACT-CHAR	BUD-CHAR	PRI-CHAR
ACT-SYRA	BUD-SYRA	PRI-SYRA

130
THE KISS PRINCIPLE

EXHIBIT 8.2 Brance profit and loss statements—systems overview

---

INPUT MODELS   DISK FILES   OUTPUT MODELS   OUTPUT REPORTS

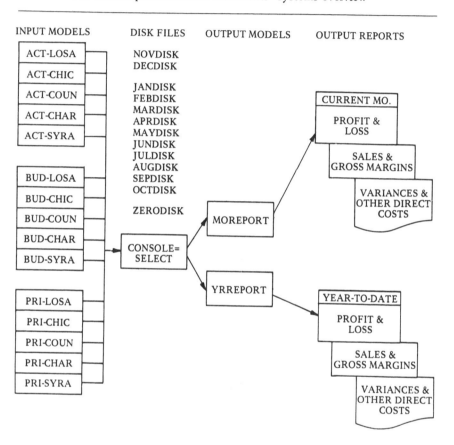

The actual models are updated on a monthly basis, and the budget and prior year models are updated on a yearly basis. See Exhibit 8.3 for a listing (DISPLAY SOURCE) of ACT-LOSA. With the exception of model name, report title, and identification (ID), all 15 input models have the same lines and logic and all were created from one master input model. Using a master input model saves a lot of time versus setting up 15 individual input models.

Below is the standard report format always found in a DISPLAY SOURCE:

1. PE or PERIODS command is used to set the number of columns to be used within the model matrix. This should be the first command to be used in building a model.

2. PAGE command applies to the printing of reports. PAGE parameters are used to define the number of lines per page, the maximum number of print positions across the page, the number of columns per report page, and the number of print characters per column and line name.

3. HE or HEADINGS command is used to insert titles over all columns found within a model.

4. RE or REPORT command defines the line number range, column number range, and the report titles.

5. DATE command is the input date or time frame that the model is being used. This information appears in the upper left-hand corner of each page.

6. ID or IDENTIFICATION command is an optional field that can be used for any purpose. This informa-

EXHIBIT 8.3

DISPLAY SOURCE
FILENAME: ACT-LOSA

PE - 23, MAX NO. LINES - 458 CURR. NO. LINES - 39 CURR. NO. RELS - 1
PAGE LENGTH 0 WIDTH 130 COLS 13 CHARS 8 NAMES 16 MESS
HE T COL 1 '   NOV ' '   · DEC ' '   JAN ' '   FEB ' '   MAR ' '   APR ' >
'   MAY ' '   JUN ' '   JUL ' '   AUG '
HE T COL 11 '   SEP ' '   OCT ' '   TOTAL YR '   'DEC YTD '   'JAN YTD '   'FEB YTD ' >
'MAR YTD '   'APR YTD '   'MAY YTD '   'JUN YTD '
HE T COL 21   'JUL YTD '   'AUG YTD '   'SEP YTD '
RE 1 L 1 T 999.9 COL 1 T 13 'ACTUAL INPUT '   'FOR LOS ANGELES '
DATE '4-1-78
ID 'ACT-LOSA
L   29.8 'VARIABLE INPUT '
L   29.9
L   30 'SHRINKAGE ' 0 0 0 0 0 0 0 0 0 0 0 0 0 0 0 0 0 0 0 0 0 0 0 0
L   50 'OBSOLESCENCE ' 0 0 0 0 0 0 0 0 0 0 0 0 0 0 0 0 0 0 0 0 0 0 0 0
L   70 'CHANGE IN STDS ' 0 0 0 0 0 0 0 0 0 0 0 0 0 0 0 0 0 0 0 0 0 0 0 0
L 150 'PURCHASE VARIABL ' 0 0 0 0 0 0 0 0 0 0 0 0 0 0 0 0 0 0 0 0 0 0 0 0
L 170 'RATE CHANGES ' 0 0 0 0 0 0 0 0 0 0 0 0 0 0 0 0 0 0 0 0 0 0 0 0
L 190 'COST OVER STD RE ' 0 0 0 0 0 0 0 0 0 0 0 0 0 0 0 0 0 0 0 0 0 0 0 0
L 269.7
L 269.8 'SALES INPUT '
L 269.9
L 270 'UNITS-TRAILERS ' 0 0 0 0 0 0 0 0 0 0 0 0 0 0 0 0 0 0 0 0 0 0 0 0
L 275 'TRUCKS ' 0 0 0 0 0 0 0 0 0 0 0 0 0 0 0 0 0 0 0 0 0 0 0
L 280 'USED ' 0 0 0 0 0 0 0 0 0 0 0 0 0 0 0 0 0 0 0 0 0 0 0
L 300 'SRO - LABOR ' 0 0 0 0 0 0 0 0 0 0 0 0 0 0 0 0 0 0 0 0 0 0 0
L 305 'INSTALLATION ' 0 0 0 0 0 0 0 0 0 0 0 0 0 0 0 0 0 0 0 0 0 0 0 0
L 310 'PARTS ' 0 0 0 0 0 0 0 0 0 0 0 0 0 0 0 0 0 0 0 0 0 0 0
L 330 'PARTS - DEALERS ' 0 0 0 0 0 0 0 0 0 0 0 0 0 0 0 0 0 0 0 0 0 0 0 0
L 335 'BRANCH CUST ' 0 0 0 0 0 0 0 0 0 0 0 0 0 0 0 0 0 0 0 0 0 0 0
L 340 'BRANCH DEALERS ' 0 0 0 0 0 0 0 0 0 0 0 0 0 0 0 0 0 0 0 0 0 0 0 0
L 394 'GROSS MARGINS '
L 395 'UNITS-TRAILERS ' 0 0 0 0 0 0 0 0 0 0 0 0 0 0 0 0 0 0 0 0 0 0 0 0
L 405 'TRUCKS ' 0 0 0 0 0 0 0 0 0 0 0 0 0 0 0 0 0 0 0 0 0 0 0
L 415 'USED ' 0 0 0 0 0 0 0 0 0 0 0 0 0 0 0 0 0 0 0 0 0
L 450 'SRO - LABOR ' 0 0 0 0 0 0 0 0 0 0 0 0 0 0 0 0 0 0 0 0 0 0 0
L 460 'INSTALLATIONS ' 0 0 0 0 0 0 0 0 0 0 0 0 0 0 0 0 0 0 0 0 0 0 0
L 470 'PARTS ' 0 0 0 0 0 0 0 0 0 0 0 0 0 0 0 0 0 0 0 0 0 0 0
L 505 'PARTS-DEALERS ' 0 0 0 0 0 0 0 0 0 0 0 0 0 0 0 0 0 0 0 0 0 0 0
L 515 'BRANCH CUST ' 0 0 0 0 0 0 0 0 0 0 0 0 0 0 0 0 0 0 0 0 0 0 0
L 525 'BRANCH DEALERS ' 0 0 0 0 0 0 0 0 0 0 0 0 0 0 0 0 0 0 0 0 0 0 0 0
L 749.7
L 749.8 'P & L INPUT '
L 749.9
L 750 'BR EXP - GROSS ' 0 0 0 0 0 0 0 0 0 0 0 0 0 0 0 0 0 0 0 0 0 0 0
L 770 'SRO BURDEN ABSOR ' 0 0 0 0 0 0 0 0 0 0 0 0 0 0 0 0 0 0 0 0 0 0 0 0
L 790 'GEN & ADMIN ' 0 0 0 0 0 0 0 0 0 0 0 0 0 0 0 0 0 0 0 0 0 0 0
L 850 'OTHER INCOME NET ' 0 0 0 0 0 0 0 0 0 0 0 0 0 0 0 0 0 0 0 0 0 0 0 0
L 860 '10% HAND CHG WAR ' 0 0 0 0 0 0 0 0 0 0 0 0 0 0 0 0 0 0 0 0 0 0 0 0
L 999 'GRAND TOTAL ' = L 30 T 860

```
COL  13 = COL  1  T  12
COL  14 = COL  1  T  2
COL  15 = COL  1  T  3
COL  16 = COL  1  T  4
COL  17 = COL  1  T  5
COL  18 = COL  1  T  6
COL  19 = COL  1  T  7
COL  20 = COL  1  T  8
COL  21 = COL  1  T  9
COL  22 = COL  1  T  10
COL  23 = COL  1  T  11
```

tion appears in the upper right-hand corner of each page. A good habit to get into is to have the model name be the ID.

7. L or LINE definitions are made up of three types of lines: title lines only, input data lines (have zero values in Exhibit 8.3), and relationship (using equal signs) lines.

8. COL or COLUMN definitions are made up of column relationships.

DISK FILES

There is a disk file for each month of the year. The first month of the fiscal year for the Smith Transport Company is November. The following are the names of the monthly disk files:

NOVDISK	FEBDISK	MAYDISK	AUGDISK
DECDISK	MARDISK	JUNDISK	SEPDISK
JANDISK	APRDISK	JULDISK	OCTDISK

See Exhibit 8.4 for a listing of JANDISK. With the exception of disk file name and column number (column 3 rep-

---

EXHIBIT 8.4

JANDISK LIST
100 CONSOLSELECT FORMAT MOREPORT
110 ACT-LOSA
120 3 1
130 NOMORE
140 BUD-LOSA
150 3 2
160 NOMORE
170 PRI-LOSA
180 3 3
190 NOMORE
200 ACT-CHIC
210 3 4
220 NOMORE
230 BUD-CHIC
240 3 5
250 NOMORE
260 PRI-CHIC
270 3 6
280 NOMORE
290 ACT-COUN
300 3 7
310 NOMORE
320 BUD-COUN
330 3 8
340 NOMORE
350 PRI-COUN
360 3 9
370 NOMORE
380 ACT-CHAR
390 3 10
400 NOMORE
410 BUD-CHAR
420 3 11
430 NOMORE
440 PRI-CHAR
450 3 12
460 NOMORE
461 ACT-SYRA
462 3 13
463 NO MORE
464 BUD-SYRA
465 3 14

570 CONSOLSELECT FORMAT YRREPORT
580 ACT-LOSA
590 15 1
600 NO MORE
610 BUD-LOSA
620 15 2
630 NOMORE
640 PRI-LOSA
650 15 3
660 NOMORE
670 ACT-CHIC
680 15 4
690 NOMORE
700 BUD-CHIC
710 15 5
720 NOMORE
730 PRI-CHIC
740 15 6
750 NOMOPE
760 ACT-COUN
770 15 7
780 NOMORE
790 BUD-COUN
800 15 8
810 NOMORE
820 PRI-COUN
830 15 9
840 NOMORE
850 ACT-CHAR
860 15 10
870 NOMORE
880 BUD-CHAR
890 15 11
900 NOMORE
910 PRI-CHAR
920 15 12
930 NOMORE
931 ACT-SYRA
932 15 13
933 NO MORE
934 BUD-SYRA
935 15 14

466 NO MORE		936 NO MORE	
467 PRI-SYRA		937 PRI-SYRA	
468 3 15		938 15 15	
469 NO MORE		939 NO MORE	
470 NOMORE		940 NOMORE	
500 REPLACE >		970 REPLACE >	
510 MOREPORT		980 YRREPORT	
520 WRITER CALCULATE 2 TIMES		990 WRITER CALCULATE 2 TIMES	
530 P&LRPT2 REPORT 1		1000 P&LRPT2 REPORT 1	
540 P&LRPT2 REPORT 2		1010 P&LRPT2 REPORT 2	
550 P&LRPT2 REPORT 3		1020 P&LRPT2 REPORT 3	
560 NOMORE		1030 NOMORE	

resents January and column 15 represents January year-to-date) commands, all 12 disk files have the same lines and logic. All 12 were created from one master disk file versus setting up 12 individual disk files.

The first-half logic of the JANDISK disk file is to select column 3 (January) from the 15 input models and save the data in an output model called MOREPORT. After this is completed, the monthly output reports are printed.

The second-half logic is a mirror image of the first-half logic. The exception is that column 15 (January year-to-date) is being selected and saved in an output model called YRREPORT. After this is completed, the year-to-date output reports are printed.

There is a thirteenth disk file called ZERODISK. This file is executed after the last yearly reports are printed in October and before the November updating of the five actual input models. This disk file moves the data from the five actual input models into its corresponding prior year input models. The next step is to zero-out the five actual input models and the five budget input models. The last step is to enter manually the yearly budget data into the five budget input models.

OUTPUT MODELS

In Exhibit 8.5, part (b) is a continuation of part (a), and part (c) is a continuation of part (b). The listing is a DISPLAY SOURCE of the output model called YRREPORT. With the exception of model name, report titles, and identification (ID), both output models have the same lines and logic. Also, both output models were created from one master output model.

The standard report format is the same as the input models. YRREPORT and MOREPORT output models both have the same three reports defined within each model.

OUTPUT REPORTS

The following are the six output report titles:

"Profit and Loss"—monthly and year-to-date

"Sales and Gross Margins"—monthly and year-to-date

"Variances and Other Direct Costs"—monthly and year-to-date

See Exhibit 8.6 for a consolidated output report.

Exhibit 8.7 is a listing of a report generator that is used to edit the six output reports. The editing is used to change the standard report format found within the output models. This listing defines the heading titles for each column, column widths, commas to separate thousands and print suppression of leading zeros.

EXHIBIT 8.5a

DISPLAY SOURCE
FILENAME: YRREPORT

```
PE - 18, MAX NO. LINES - 578 CURR. NO. LINES - 121 CURR. NO. RELS - 34
PAGE LENGTH   0 WIDTH   130 COLS   13 CHARS   8 NAMES   16 MESS
HE T COL 1 '——L'      'OS ANGEL'     'ES—'      '——'      '-CHICAGO'      '——' >
'—COU'    'NCIL BLU'    'FFS—'    '——'
HE T COL 11 'CHARLOTT'     'E—'      '—CO'    'NSOLIDAT'    'ED—'
HE M COL 1  'ACTUAL'  'BUDGET'  'PRIOR YR'  'ACTUAL'  'BUDGET'  'PRIOR YR' >
'ACTUAL'    'BUDGET'    'PRIOR YR'    'ACTUAL'
HE M COL 11  'BUDGET'    'PRIOR YR'    'ACTUAL'    'BUDGET    'PRIOR YR'
RE 1 L 1 T 250 COL 1 T 15'        SMITH TRANSPORT COMPANY' >
'VARIANCES AND OTHER DIRECT COSTS'
RE 2 L 250 T 600 COL 1 T 15'        SMITH TRANSPORT COMPANY' >
' SALES AND GROSS MARGINS '
RE 3 L 601 T 999.9 COL 1 T 15'        SMITH TRANSPORT COMPANY' >
' PROFIT AND LOSS'
DATE 'FOR JUN 1979 YTD'
ID 'YRREPORT       '
L   1    'VARIANCE REPORT' SUP
L  10    'OTHER DIRECT:'
L  20
L  30   ' SHRINKAGE' 0 0 0 0 0 0 0 0 0 0 0 0 0 0 0 0 0
L  40
L  50   ' OBSOLESCENCE' 0 0 0 0 0 0 0 0 0 0 0 0 0 0 0 0 0 0
L  60
L  70   ' CHANGE IN STDS' 0 0 0 0 0 0 0 0 0 0 0 0 0 0 0 0 0
L  80
L  90   '-'
L 100   'TOT OTHER DIRECT  = L 30 + L 50 + L 70
L 110
L 120
L 130   'VARIANCES:'
L 140
L 150   '  PURCHASE' 0 0 0 0 0 0 0 0 0 0 0 0 0 0 0 0 0
L 160
L 170   '  RATE CHANGES' 0 0 0 0 0 0 0 0 0 0 0 0 0 0 0 0 0
L 180
L 190   '  OVER STD REBLD' 0 0 0 0 0 0 0 0 0 0 0 0 0 0 0 0 0
L 200
L 210   '-'
L 220   'TOTAL VARIANCES' = L 150 + L 170 + L 190
L 230   '='
L 251   'SALES REPORT' SUP
L 260   'GROSS SALES:'
L 265
L 270   'UNITS-TRAILERS' 0 0 0 0 0 0 0 0 0 0 0 0 0 0 0 0 0
L 275   '        -TRUCKS' 0 0 0 0 0 0 0 0 0 0 0 0 0 0 0 0 0
L 280   '        -USED' 0 0 0 0 0 0 0 0 0 0 0 0 0 0 0 0 0
```

EXHIBIT 8.5b

```
L  285 '-'
L  290 'TOTAL UNITS' = L 270 + L 275 + L 280
L  295
L  300 'SRO-LABOR' 0 0 0 0 0 0 0 0 0 0 0 0 0 0 0 0 0 0
L  305 '     -INSTALLATION' 0 0 0 0 0 0 0 0 0 0 0 0 0 0 0 0 0 0 0
L  310 '     -PARTS' 0 0 0 0 0 0 0 0 0 0 0 0 0 0 0 0 0 0
L  315 '-'
L  320 'TOTAL SRO' = L 300 + L 305 + L 310
L  325
L  330 'PARTS-DEALERS' 0 0 0 0 0 0 0 0 0 0 0 0 0 0 0 0 0 0
L  335 '        -BR CUST' 0 0 0 0 0 0 0 0 0 0 0 0 0 0 0 0 0 0
L  340 '        -BR DEALERS' 0 0 0 0 0 0 0 0 0 0 0 0 0 0 0 0 0 0
L  345 '-'
L  350 'TOTAL PARTS' = L 330 + L 335 + L 340
L  355 '-'
L  360 'TOTAL SALES' = L 290 + L 320 + L 350
```

```
L  370
L  375
L  380
L  385 'GROSS MARGINS:'
L  390
L  395 'UNITS-TRAILERS' 0 0 0 0 0 0 0 0 0 0 0 0 0 0 0 0 0 0
L  400 '     -% OF SALES'  DEC 1 = 100 * L 395 / L 270
L  405 '        -TRUCKS' 0 0 0 0 0 0 0 0 0 0 0 0 0 0 0 0 0 0
L  410 '     -% OF SALES' DEC 1 = 100 * L 405 / L 275
L  415 '        -USED' 0 0 0 0 0 0 0 0 0 0 0 0 0 0 0 0 0 0
L  420 '     -% OF SALES' DEC 1 = 100 * L 415 / L 280
L  425 '-'
L  430 'TOTAL UNITS' = L 395 + L 405 + L 415
L  435 '     -% OF SALES'  DEC 1 = 100 * L 430 / L 290
L  440 '-'
L  445
L  450 'SRO-LABOR' 0 0 0 0 0 0 0 0 0 0 0 0 0 0 0 0 0 0
L  455 '     -% OF SALES' DEC 1 = 100 * L 450 / L 300
L  460 '     -INSTALLATION' 0 0 0 0 0 0 0 0 0 0 0 0 0 0 0 0 0 0 0
L  465 '     -% OF SALES' DEC 1 = 100 * L 460 / L 305
L  470 '     -PARTS' 0 0 0 0 0 0 0 0 0 0 0 0 0 0 0 0 0 0
L  475 '     -% OF SALES' DEC 1 = 100 * L 470 / L 310
L  480 '-'
L  485 'TOTAL SRO' = L 450 + L 460 + L 470
L  490 '     -% OF SALES' DEC 1 = 100 * L 485 / L 320
L  495 '-'
L  500
L  505 'PARTS-DEALERS' 0 0 0 0 0 0 0 0 0 0 0 0 0 0 0 0 0 0
L  510 '     -% OF SALES' DEC 1 = 100 * L 505 / L 330
L  515 '        -BR CUST' 0 0 0 0 0 0 0 0 0 0 0 0 0 0 0 0 0 0
```

EXHIBIT 8.5b (continued)

```
L   520 '    -% OF SALES' DEC 1 =  100 * L 515 / L 335
L   525 '     -BR DEALERS' 0 0 0 0 0 0 0 0 0 0 0 0 0 0 0 0 0 0
L   530 '    -% OF SALES' DEC 1 =  100 * L 525 / L 340
L   535 '-'
L   540 'TOTAL PARTS' =  L 505 + L 515 + L 525
L   545 '    -% OF SALES' DEC 1 =  100 * L 540 / L 350
L   550 '-'
L   555
L   560 '-'
L   565 'TOTAL GROSS MARG' =  L 430 + L 485 + L 540
L   570 '    -% OF SALES' DEC 1 =  100 * L 565 / L 360
L   575 '-'
L   601 'P & L REPORT'  SUP
L   610 'GROSS SALES' =  L 360
L   620
L   630 'GROSS MARGIN-STD' =  L 565
L   640 '    % OF SALES' DEC 1 =  100 * L 630 / L 610
L   650 '-'
L   660
L   670 'OTHER DIRECT' =  L 100
L   680
L   690 'VARIANCES' =  L 220
L   700 '-'
L   710 '    'GROSS MARGIN-ACT' =  L 630 + L 670 + L 690
L   720 '    % OF SALES'  DEC 1 =  100 * L 710 / L 610
L   730 '-'
L   740
L   750 'BRANCH EXP-GROSS' 0 0 0 0 0 0 0 0 0 0 0 0 0 0 0 0 0 0
L   760
L   770 'SRO BURDEN ABSOR' 0 0 0 0 0 0 0 0 0 0 0 0 0 0 0 0 0 0
L   780
L   790 'GEN & ADMIN-2.3%' 0 0 0 0 0 0 0 0 0 0 0 0 0 0 0 0 0 0
L   800 '-'
L   810 'TOTAL EXP-NET' =  L 750 + L 770 + L 790
L   820 '    % OF SALES' DEC 1 =  100 * L 810 / L 610
L   840
L   850 'OTHER INCOME-NET' 0 0 0 0 0 0 0 0 0 0 0 0 0 0 0 0 0 0
L   855
L   860 '15% HAND CHG-WAR' 0 0 0 0 0 0 0 0 0 0 0 0 0 0 0 0 0 0
L   865 '-'
L   870 'P&L BEFORE TAXES' =  L 710 - L 810 + L 850 + L 860
L   880 '    % OF SALES' DEC 1 =  100 * L 870 / L 610
L   890 '-'
```

EXHIBIT 8.5c

COL 16	L	1	T 395	=	COL 1	+	COL 4	+	COL 7	+	COL 10	+	COL 13
COL 16	L	405	T 405	=	COL 1	+	COL 4	+	COL 7	+	COL 10	+	COL 13
COL 16	L	415	T 415	=	COL 1	+	COL 4	+	COL 7	+	COL 10	+	COL 13
COL 16	L	425	T 430	=	COL 1	+	COL 4	+	COL 7	+	COL 10	+	COL 13
COL 16	L	440	T 450	=	COL 1	+	COL 4	+	COL 7	+	COL 10	+	COL 13
COL 16	L	460	T 460	=	COL 1	+	COL 4	+	COL 7	+	COL 10	+	COL 13
COL 16	L	470	T 470	=	COL 1	+	COL 4	+	COL 7	+	COL 10	+	COL 13
COL 16	L	480	T 485	=	COL 1	+	COL 4	+	COL 7	+	COL 10	+	COL 13
COL 16	L	495	T 505	=	COL 1	+	COL 4	+	COL 7	+	COL 10	+	COL 13
COL 16	L	515	T 515	=	COL 1	+	COL 4	+	COL 7	+	COL 10	+	COL 13
COL 16	L	525	T 525	=	COL 1	+	COL 4	+	COL 7	+	COL 10	+	COL 13
COL 16	L	535	T 540	=	COL 1	+	COL 4	+	COL 7	+	COL 10	+	COL 13
COL 16	L	550	T 565	=	COL 1	+	COL 4	+	COL 7	+	COL 10	+	COL 13
COL 16	L	575	T 630	=	COL 1	+	COL 4	+	COL 7	+	COL 10	+	COL 13
COL 16	L	650	T 710	=	COL 1	+	COL 4	+	COL 7	+	COL 10	+	COL 13
COL 16	L	730	T 810	=	COL 1	+	COL 4	+	COL 7	+	COL 10	+	COL 13
COL 16	L	830	T 870	=	COL 1	+	COL 4	+	COL 7	+	COL 10	+	COL 13
COL 17	L	1	T 395	=	COL 2	+	COL 5	+	COL 8	+	COL 11	+	COL 14
COL 17	L	405	T 405	=	COL 2	+	COL 5	+	COL 8	+	COL 11	+	COL 14
COL 17	L	415	T 415	=	COL 2	+	COL 5	+	COL 8	+	COL 11	+	COL 14
COL 17	L	425	T 430	=	COL 2	+	COL 5	+	COL 8	+	COL 11	+	COL 14
COL 17	L	440	T 450	=	COL 2	+	COL 5	+	COL 8	+	COL 11	+	COL 14
COL 17	L	460	T 460	=	COL 2	+	COL 5	+	COL 8	+	COL 11	+	COL 14
COL 17	L	470	T 470	=	COL 2	+	COL 5	+	COL 8	+	COL 11	+	COL 14

COL 14	+ COL 11	+ COL 8	+ COL 5	+ COL 2	=	480	T	485	L	COL 17
COL 14	+ COL 11	+ COL 8	+ COL 5	+ COL 2	=	495	T	505	L	COL 17
COL 14	+ COL 11	+ COL 8	+ COL 5	+ COL 2	=	515	T	515	L	COL 17
COL 14	+ COL 11	+ COL 8	+ COL 5	+ COL 2	=	525	T	525	L	COL 17
COL 14	+ COL 11	+ COL 8	+ COL 5	+ COL 2	=	535	T	540	L	COL 17
COL 14	+ COL 11	+ COL 8	+ COL 5	+ COL 2	=	550	T	565	L	COL 17
COL 14	+ COL 11	+ COL 8	+ COL 5	+ COL 2	=	575	T	630	L	COL 17
COL 14	+ COL 11	+ COL 8	+ COL 5	+ COL 2	=	650	T	710	L	COL 17
COL 14	+ COL 11	+ COL 8	+ COL 5	+ COL 2	=	730	T	810	L	COL 17
COL 15	+ COL 12	+ COL 8	+ COL 5	+ COL 2	=	830	T	870	L	COL 18
COL 15	+ COL 12	+ COL 9	+ COL 6	+ COL 3	=	1	T	395	L	COL 18
COL 15	+ COL 12	+ COL 9	+ COL 6	+ COL 3	=	405	T	405	L	COL 18
COL 15	+ COL 12	+ COL 9	+ COL 6	+ COL 3	=	415	T	415	L	COL 18
COL 15	+ COL 12	+ COL 9	+ COL 6	+ COL 3	=	425	T	430	L	COL 18
COL 15	+ COL 12	+ COL 9	+ COL 6	+ COL 3	=	440	T	450	L	COL 18
COL 15	+ COL 12	+ COL 9	+ COL 6	+ COL 3	=	460	T	460	L	COL 18
COL 15	+ COL 12	+ COL 9	+ COL 6	+ COL 3	=	470	T	470	L	COL 18
COL 15	+ COL 12	+ COL 9	+ COL 6	+ COL 3	=	480	T	485	L	COL 18
COL 15	+ COL 12	+ COL 9	+ COL 6	+ COL 3	=	495	T	505	L	COL 18
COL 15	+ COL 12	+ COL 9	+ COL 6	+ COL 3	=	515	T	515	L	COL 18
COL 15	+ COL 12	+ COL 9	+ COL 6	+ COL 3	=	525	T	525	L	COL 18
COL 15	+ COL 12	+ COL 9	+ COL 6	+ COL 3	=	535	T	540	L	COL 18
COL 15	+ COL 12	+ COL 9	+ COL 6	+ COL 3	=	550	T	565	L	COL 18
COL 15	+ COL 12	+ COL 9	+ COL 6	+ COL 3	=	575	T	630	L	COL 18
COL 15	+ COL 12	+ COL 9	+ COL 6	+ COL 3	=	650	T	710	L	COL 18
COL 15	+ COL 12	+ COL 9	+ COL 6	+ COL 3	=	730	T	810	L	COL 18
COL 15	+ COL 12	+ COL 9	+ COL 6	+ COL 3	=	830	T	870	L	COL 18

EXHIBIT 8.6

SMITH TRANSPORT COMPANY
VARIANCES AND OTHER DIRECT COSTS

FOR JUN 1979 YTD   YRREPORT

LINE NO		LOS ANGELES			CHICAGO			COUNCIL BLUFFS		
		ACTUAL	BUDGET	PRIOR YR	ACTUAL	BUDGET	PRIOR YR	ACTUAL	BUDGET	PRIOR YR
10.0	OTHER DIRECT:									
20.0										
30.0	SHRINKAGE	-3,235	-3,235	-3,210	-1,941	-1,941	-1,270	-1,294	-1,294	-1,900
40.0										
50.0	OBSOLESCENCE	-3,330	-3,235	-3,250	-1,998	-1,941	-1,300	-1,998	-1,941	-2,966
60.0										
70.0	CHANGE IN STDS	9,220	5,000	6,464	4,393	4,000	3,665	8,499	4,500	3,831
80.0										
90.0										
100.0	TOT OTHER DIRECT	2,655	-1,470	4	454	118	1,095	5,207	1,265	-1,035
110.0										
120.0										
130.0	VARIANCES:									
140.0										
150.0	PURCHASE	-956	-328	312	-982	200	-796	-244	1,664	1,306
160.0										
170.0	RATE CHANGES									
180.0										
190.0	OVER STD REBLD	-1,376	-3,664	-4,689	-1,002	-1,328	-1,272	-735	-328	-305
200.0										
210.0										
220.0	TOTAL VARIANCES	-2,332	-3,992	-4,377	-1,984	-1,128	-2,068	-979	1,336	1,001
230.0										

SMITH TRANSPORT COMPANY
VARIANCES AND OTHER DIRECT COSTS

FOR JUN 1979 YTD

YRREPORT

LINE NO		----- CHARLOTTE -----			----- SYRACUSE -----			----- CONSOLIDATED -----		
		ACTUAL	BUDGET	PRIOR YR	ACTUAL	BUDGET	PRIOR YR	ACTUAL	BUDGET	PRIOR YR
10.0	OTHER DIRECT:									
20.0										
30.0	SHRINKAGE	-1,941	-1,941	-1,270	-1,500	-1,500		-9,911	-9,911	-7,650
40.0										
50.0	OBSOLESCENCE	-666	-647	-1,300	-500	-500		-8,492	-8,264	-8,816
60.0										
70.0	CHANGE IN STDS	4,349	2,000	1,198				26,461	15,500	15,158
80.0										
90.0										
100.0	TOT OTHER DIRECT	1,742	-588	-1,372	-2,000	-2,000		8,058	-2,675	-1,308
110.0										
120.0										
130.0	VARIANCES:									
140.0										
150.0	PURCHASE	23	-664					-2,159	872	822
160.0										
170.0	RATE CHANGES	1,507						1,507		
180.0										
190.0	OVER STD REBLD	-643	-664			-500		-3,756	-6,484	-6,266
200.0										
210.0										
220.0	TOTAL VARIANCES	887	-1,328		-500	-500		-4,408	-5,612	-5,444
230.0										

EXHIBIT 8.7

P&LRPT2   LIST

LISTING OF REPORT FILE P&LRPT2   (::::)

TITLES

HEADINGS

COL	1	- - - - - -
		ACTUAL
COL	2	LOS ANGELES
		BUDGET
COL	3	- - - - - -
		PRIOR YR
COL	4	- - - - - -
		ACTUAL
COL	5	- -CHICAGO- -
		BUDGET
COL	6	- - - - - -
		PRIOR YR
COL	7	- - - - - C
		ACTUAL
COL	8	OUNCIL BLUF
		BUDGET
COL	9	FS- - - -
		PRIOR YR
COL	10	- - - - - -
		ACTUAL
COL	11	-CHARLOTTE-
		BUDGET
COL	12	- - - - - -
		PRIOR YR
COL	13	- - - - - -
		ACTUAL
COL	14	- SYRACUSE- -
		BUDGET
COL	15	- - - - - -
		PRIOR YR

EXHIBIT 8.7 (continued)

```
COL     16              - - - - - -
                        ACTUAL
COL     17        CONSOLIDATE
                        BUDGET
COL     18        D- - - - -
                        PRIOR YR
NON  STD    COLUMN  WIDTHS
COL      1  WIDTH  11  CHARS
COL      2  WIDTH  11  CHARS
COL      3  WIDTH  11  CHARS
COL      4  WIDTH  11  CHARS
COL      5  WIDTH  11  CHARS
COL      6  WIDTH  11  CHARS
COL      7  WIDTH  11  CHARS
COL      8  WIDTH  11  CHARS
COL      9  WIDTH  11  CHARS
COL     10  WIDTH  11  CHARS
COL     11  WIDTH  11  CHARS
COL     12  WIDTH  11  CHARS
COL     13  WIDTH  11  CHARS
COL     14  WIDTH  11  CHARS
COL     15  WIDTH  11  CHARS
COL     16  WIDTH  11  CHARS
COL     17  WIDTH  11  CHARS
COL     18  WIDTH  11  CHARS
SELECTED LINES
* * * * * * * * * * * * *
-ALL LINES IN MODEL
SELECTED COLUMNS
* * * * * * * * * * * * * * *
COL   1  TO  18  EDITING   ,Z
LINE NUMBERS PRINTED
PAGE NUMBERS SUPPRESSED
TITLES PRINTED ON ALL PAGES
SYSTEM CALCULATES COLS/PAGE
*** END OF REPORT LISTING ***
```

Benefits

Before the INSIGHT system was implemented, it took users 40 manual hours per month to produce the branch profit and loss statements. Now it takes four hours a month using INSIGHT—a 90% reduction in time. Also, the computer reports look more professional than handwritten reports and were done right the first time.

The two main benefits of using INSIGHT are the savings in manual time and the fact that it is a great management tool. In addition, INSIGHT systems are flexible enough to grow with.

INSIGHT language has been in use for many years and has continuously been maintained and improved to meet user demands. Approximately each year, INSIGHT comes out with a new version of their software package. The new version is made up of new commands, enhancements to pre-existing commands, and better processing efficiency, making INSIGHT a good proprietary software package that improves every year.

9

Data Processing
and
Word Processing

As mentioned at the beginning of chapter 8, this chapter will look at another possible alternative to the traditional data processing life cycle for business applications.

One of the hottest buzzwords today is word processing (WP). The next step beyond word processing will be joint DP/WP applications. Before looking at possible joint applications, we should look at the history of DP and WP, what they have in common, and where they are going. Therefore, let us examine the picture as to yesterday, today, and tomorrow.

NOTE: This chapter is co-authored with Mona R. Bertrand who supervises the Word Processing Center at Carrier Corporation in Syracuse, New York. She has also written articles for several WP publications and speaks at conferences on word processing and management. The author is indebted to Mona.

Yesterday

WORD PROCESSING

The closest thing to WP, as we know it now, consisted of the all too familiar boss–secretary configuration. On a typical day, the secretary had the opportunity of "processing" approximately 10 letters in final forms, sandwiched between answering the telephone, making photocopies, bringing the boss and coworkers coffee, etc.

The human aspect at that time was ultimately highlighted and very much in evidence. Unfortunately, this arrangement did not promote efficiency nor did anything in the way of advancing technology or a secretary's method of getting work done. The electric typewriter was the secretary's only tool. The skills learned in high school or secretarial college were the only ones he or she was allowed to utilize, and the chances of getting a better position or updating his or her technology were nil.

The workload in an individual office peaked so that emergency deadlines found the secretary frustrated and indulging in copious amounts of correction fluid and correction tape and eraser crumbs jamming the typewriter, only to be met the following week by perhaps another emergency or, worse yet, a few days of very little to do. There was no leveling of workloads and no one to share responsibilities, only the grim determinaiton to go it alone.

Automation in the office was unheard of. Factories and DP had undergone a dramatic change, but the office remained essentially the same as it had been for 100 years when the typewriter had been invented. The secretary re-

EXHIBIT 9.1 Word processing yesterday

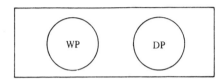

mained the "office wife" and until the advent of WP, as we know it now, any deviation of that role was unlikely and unheard of.

DATA PROCESSING

Early 1960s. Most systems were stand-alone, noncompatible systems located at major operating units. Major applications were in the area of financial reporting. Mass storage devices began to be adopted widely, but magnetic tape was still the primary medium for storage of the data files.

Late 1960s. Most systems were becoming stand-alone, compatible systems and the software was becoming standardized. New applications were in the area of financial control. There was a more extensive use of data communications. Mass storage devices were much larger, providing storage for billions of characters of data on-line to the computer.

This was the era of decentralization, the advantages of which were as follows:

Improved effectiveness

Lighter economic consequences due to failure

Less training and bureaucracy

Less competition for service

Less sophistication needed

Lower communication costs

Early 1970s. During the early part of the decade we began to see the concentration of processing power at control sites with terminal access to large control databases. New applications were in the areas of order entry and inventory.

This is the era of centralization. The following were the advantages of centralization:

Lower overall cost of equipment and systems development cost

Fewer personnel problems and support personnel

Better DP cost control

More sophisticated systems possible

Ability to run large jobs

Today

WORD PROCESSING

WP is separated from DP by only a thin line of technology. Though some WP centers are sponsored by the DP departments of large corporations, WP is still looked upon as unique in its stature and makeup.

Currently, first and foremost, WP is people. These people possess special talents, coupled with a spirit of adventure,

EXHIBIT 9.2 Word processing today

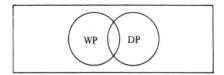

and have ultimately conquered their fear of change along with subsequent acquisition of certain skills. WP personnel are accustomed to an atmosphere where nothing "stands still," where today's adequate station may be obsolete tomorrow. In a WP center utilization of the latest and most modern automated and computerized typing equipment, as well as efficient machine dictation, is a way of life.

Human resource requirements in this specialized field include a willingness to share technology and the patience to do so. One highly noticeable characteristic of most WP people is their complete knowledge of the systems with which they work, along with their patience and exceptional willingness to get the job done. In essence, they speak the specialized languages of the systems. In addition, as a matter of course they are expected to pitch in to teach others in the corporation as well as new center personnel the methods of gaining the most efficient productivity from this highly specialized equipment. As part of the daily routine, they fully employ the WP work-sharing and teamwork concepts.

Contrary to popular belief, the WP function is not an isolated one within the corporate organization. There exists not only the normal amount of interpersonal relationships and

day-to-day stresses and strains found in most other departments, but due to the overlapping scope of endeavors, WP
people handle situations and cope with more varieties of
personalities than most other departments ever do.

Yet, a great many more talents are required of the WP
operator other than being capable of dealing effectively with
people, handling sophisticated typing equipment, and training others. There is an overriding requirement to select people with a flair for writing procedures and training manuals,
and with the foresight and cognizance to make equipment
evaluations. Moreover, superior editorial skills are required—
that innate, anticipatory power to interpret vague references, to rearrange, to reemphasize, to restructure, to make
clear.

Among the attributes of a good word processor is, as already mentioned, patience—the patience to deal with a
highly motivated perfectionist, the individual who not only
wants the work done on time, but also wants it to be letter-
perfect.

The ability to select new equipment, evaluate it, and actively participate in subsequent training programs is an in-
herent requirement of WP personnel. This ability is an on-
going process because the technology is constantly changing
and being updated at an accelerated rate. Yet, mere accep-
tance, knowledge, and evaluation are not enough. The ability
to fit the new pieces of equipment to specific jobs is perhaps
more important, the criteria always being, will it do the job,
and, if so, will the customers be satisfied with the output?

The human aspect is highlighted by the operators' pride
in their unique skills, the advanced technological environment in which they work, and their ability to produce sizable
volumes of work. The tools they have learned are highly so-

phisticated, enhancing their position within the company, as well as their own self-esteem and pride in their work. These newly acquired skills have opened up new career paths for yesterday's "mere" secretary who had only the aspiration to supervise and/or conduct training on a managerial level. Workload sharing and leveling are two of the many advantages of WP. No longer is error correction a problem, nor is revision, extensive or otherwise. Responsibility for deadlines and priorities is shared by operators who can divide a lengthy job into as many parts as necessary, and yet complete, format, and print it as one. Planning is done by a knowledgeable supervisor who knows the workload, the operators' abilities, and the capabilities of the equipment.

Indeed, today WP is people—people plus machines plus know-how. Basically, there is no comparison of today's WP concept to yesterday's boss–secretary configuration when you consider efficiency, production statistics, talent, and employee opportunities.

DATA PROCESSING

We are now seeing the beginnings of distributed data processing (DDP) which means having processing power and databases at remote locations. The new applications are transaction driven.

This is the era in which the pendulum is swinging from centralization to DDP. DDP is a cross between centralization and decentralization. With DDP, computer power is decentralized at the remote sites to capture and process data at its source and transmit large amounts of clean data to the central site. Therefore, computer power is decentralized but control of computer power is centralized. The concept of

DDP has been around for a long time, but only recently has it been possible to achieve. This move was made feasible by the development of inexpensive minicomputers and cheaper data communications.

A real DDP system is a network of powerful, self-sufficient satellite systems communicating with each other and/or the host computer. This is an environment where business information is controlled by the people using it. Data communications must be efficient and simple to add to existing data processing systems.

The following are the advantages of DDP:

User has local processing and data storage capability

User has integrated access to other computers

User controls his or her own data

Noncompetitive access to user

Reduces peak load demands on central computer power

Greater responsiveness to user

Quick support of new applications without costly additions to the central computer

Lower total system communications costs

Less training and bureaucracy

On the other side are the disadvantages of DDP:

Duplication of input, output, and functions

Higher cost due to duplication of hardware, software, data, space, and people

Application size and complexity restrictions

Possible incompatibilities

Restricted growth

More difficult management and control of operations, standards, application of development, and data bases

Empire building

Limited equipment selection expertise

Limited vendor relations/negotiating power

Tomorrow

The future will bring broader use of DDP elements and redistribution of previously centralized applications. Computers and their networks will interface with other organizations. Therefore, we shall see an overall increase in computer usage with both new and expansion of existing application areas.

Because of their expertise, DP people will help in the evaluation and selection of WP equipment. WP and DP people will be sharing the same work stations and the same communication system. Also, some WP and DP data files will be compatible.

Some work stations will be a multifunction unit with various work-keys. At a touch, a work-key could be used for word processing, source data entry, central computer inquiry, and stand-alone data processing. These multifunction units can function in work station clusters and communicate with other dispersed work station clusters and/or the host computer.

EXHIBIT 9.3 Word processing tomorrow

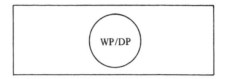

DDP + DP + DWP + WP = IP

Distributed DP plus DP plus distributed WP plus WP will be combined together for the next evolutionary jump into information processing (IP). Top management within each company will mandate this jump because they will realize the economics from sharing equipment, personnel, and data.

The following common equipment features can be used for both DP and WP.

Hardware

The hardware will be storage devices, video displays and printers. The intelligence of the hardware can be any one of the following: hard wired, microprocessor based, processing capability in a host computer, or a terminal with its own processing capability.

Software

WP software could be added to the resident DP software available which could include user-oriented application software packages that greatly expand the usefulness of the system.

Communications

Communication options can allow WP to transmit information to other dispersed work station clusters and/or the host computer. This information could become part of a database to be used in DP applications and/or transmitted back to WP for their own use.

Functions

The major function could be a service bureau. The intermediate functions could be a charge-back system and/or production statistics system. The minor functions will be create, delete, list, merge, sort, and update.

APPLICATIONS

Some of the applications that can be used are accounts receivable-past due, long texts, marketing surveys, or literature and mailing labels. Other applications would utilize the SORT function. For example, if we had 100 different catalogues on file by part number, we could select different catalogues and sort them down together by part number. Finally, we could print a new catalogue or report.

Some other uses are applications for in-plant phototypesetting and transmitting material electronically to remote locations via telecommunication modes. Most phototypeset material becomes copy for some form of duplicating or printing process. The material could be financial reports, annual summaries, booklets, pamphlets, catalogues, directories, or advertisements. In this type of arrangement the phototypesetting machine itself becomes a peripheral to be controlled by the computer.

As time goes on, we shall find many more joint applications. Some of the above applications have programs which select certain variable data and output it to WP on storage devices. Later on the variable data will be blended with the fixed data that had previously been stored on storage devices by WP.

In conclusion, WP and DP will be parts of the total corporate information system.

10
Automated Records Management System

There are many large corporations made up of different and almost independent strategy centers that have developed isolated records management procedures which include many manual systems. In particular, we shall look at one of these large corporations, Flug Incorporated. The following are some of the common shortcomings of the various records management systems throughout its six strategy centers:

Lack of uniformity in records management policies and procedures in the various record management departments.

Lack of automated indexing of records, either manual or inflexible computer listings.

Computer applications are batch, totally inflexible, and not used throughout the corporation.

Lack of standard input or output data.

Check-in and check-out system is manual,
time-consuming, and inaccurate.

Labor intensive—many clerical functions are
duplicated.

Lack of effective security control.

Only ability to measure level of file activity is
manual statistical gathering (time-consuming).

Duplicate records filed.

Cross filing of records.

Limited retrieval and update capabilities.

Continued growth in file room staff to meet
user demands.

User request not always completed in a
timely manner.

Poor utilization of office floor space.

Flug Incorporated decided to set up a corporate records
management department with a coordinator for each
strategy center. The staff included people who had at least
four-year degrees and experience in library science or computer science. Because the corporation had so many different types of records (e.g., technical, lease rentals, correspondence, and contracts) that were constantly growing
in volume, the newly formed corporate records management
staff decided the best and most productive course of action
was to purchase a library software system to run on their
host computer. The staff made up the following question-

naire/checklist to use as they went to the various software houses that specialized in library systems:

1. *Vendor Name and Location*

2. *Costs* (will need legal assistance)
   purchase
   maintenance
   lease

3. *Overall System*
   delivery dates
   trial period
   documentation
   training
   references
   expandability
   service
   communications
   compatible to host
   software updates
   report types
   initialize from tape or disk
   security access
   on-line response time
   search methods
   multiterminal updating
   file size restrictions
   backup
   conversion and installation plan

4. *Minimal System Requirements*

System that requires no more than 25% total
in-house programming.
Extensive data selection capabilities based on
Boolean and relational operators.
Expandable system (i.e., data bases).
Distributed availability with a number of terminals
capable of being used concurrently in a network.
On-line distributed data entry and data capture
at the point of origination of the document.
Responsive retrieval of information.
Simple procedure for report generation.
Built-in accuracy checks.
Security provisions to ensure data integrity.
The flexibility to add, delete, and change
data on-line.
The flexibility to easily modify the screens
and programs in order to handle new infor-
mation needs.

After reviewing approximately two dozen library software
systems, the corporate records management staff decided
that the best system for them and for the personnel in the
various file rooms was a package called Automated Records
Management System (ARMS). ARMS was purchased and
phased in at each file room location—one record type application at a time until all the various record types were implemented throughout the organization. The corporate
records management coordinator for each strategy center
played a big part in successfully implementing ARMS.

The following functions can now be performed on work stations (video-display tubes) at the various file rooms throughout the organization:

1. Produce bar code labels for new records.

2. Enter information on new records into the system.

3. Charge out a record with a bar code laser scanner that is attached to the work station. The date, time, and employee number are logged in the disk memory.

4. Record the return of a record to the file room with a bar code laser scanner that is attached to the work station.

5. Reserve a particular record for the next user.

6. Report on the location of any specific record at any time.

7. Flag records for removal to dormant storage.

8. Produce a list of records which have been checked out and not yet returned. Also, produce patron overdue notices.

9. Produce various statistical listings on circulation transactions.

10. Set up a cross-reference of particular fields (i.e., names and numbers) within a record that is defined on the database.

11. Set up search fields within a record that is defined on the database. Also, search terms can be truncated to minimize keying; for example, if we are searching under names for Mark Twain, we could enter: Twain,

Mark, Ma, M, Twai, or any portion of the name or heading that we feel will get us close enough in the file. The system will display in alphabetical or numerical order that portion of the file starting with the closest match to the search term.

12. Reference thesaurus guide-subsystem for each record type application or record series. The thesaurus guide-subsystem allows us to standardize indexing vocabulary for better retrieval performance and to enter common search terms and have them switched to preferred terms.

13. Reference INFOINDEX which is Flug's records retention reporting system (e.g., document types, retention times, and physical locations) and also the index for all of the record series. INFOINDEX was developed to assume the role of a monitoring and control tool in the administration and implementation of a uniform and sound records management program in accordance with federal laws, state laws, and corporate policies. Only the corporate records management department controls the updating of INFO-INDEX.

Finally, the most dramatic benefits of using ARMS are:

1. *Speed of checking-in and checking-out:* By using lightpens or laser scanners against bar coded records, the process of checking-in and checking-out will be performed dramatically faster than can be done manually. The daily savings in time will be approximately five minutes per record times the number of

records processed. This will help to further the relationship the corporate records management staff and file room personnel have with their users. Also, the up-to-the-minute status of every record and its contents in the system is known at all times.

2. *Automatic compilation and reporting statistics:* The system continuously updates statistical data while performing circulation transactions so that each report contains information which provides statistical reports on circulation by patron, item subject categories, daily check-outs, check-ins, and reserves placed. ARMS can produce automatically and on demand the patron overdue notices. By prompt notice to the patron of material that he or she has kept overdue, the records management department increases its chances of recovering its records.

3. *Software updates:* The software will have yearly updates which will include enhancements to existing commands, new commands, new reports, and better overall operating efficiency. ARMS has the ability to restructure the database, for example, adding new data elements to a current defined record or defining a new record type.

4. *Security controls:* ARMS has different security levels that can be predefined only by the corporate records management department for each file room location and users. The security levels include who can access what kind of data and who can update the data.

5. *Elimination of paper files:* The files for circulating . material, overdue material, reserve requests, search requests, and report sheets are eliminated.

6. *Growing with the system:* As requirements for records grow, ARMS can be upgraded to add additional storage space, processors, and user terminals to meet increased needs. Networking can take place when two or more file room locations share the same collection of data by means of reciprocal borrowing.

7. *Benefits to management:* ARMS solves the major information control problems and allows for utilization of a single system to handle all record types, rather than having multiple unrelated systems. It also provides management with needed reports, such as departmental usage, which would aid in future space, equipment, and personnel planning.

8. *Benefits to users:* By streamlining the request procedure, ARMS allows for telephone or while-you-wait or rush requests. This would increase the level of service provided to users.

9. *Benefits to the corporate records management department and file room personnel:* ARMS provides job enrichment by having an easy-to-use, easy-to-learn tool which will increase the productivity of the file room personnel by eliminating the majority of time-consuming, tedious manual filing. Also, it provides better service, which will further the relationship the corporate records management staff and file room personnel have with their users.

11

Programmable Portable Data Terminals

A company in San Diego, California, called Multiple Systems Incorporated (MSI) manufactures and markets programmable portable data terminals or hand-held computers. Most data entry applications that can be keyed-in with a sit-down video-display terminal can also be keyed-in with portable hand-held computers (see Exhibit 11.1). This allows someone to key-in the data at the source and transmit the error-free data over telephone lines (see Exhibit 11.2) to the host computer, thereby circumventing the traditional data-gathering procedure (manual data collection delivered to a central site, transcribed, and keyed into the host computer).

Below are some of the features of a hand-held computer:

Has two lines of liquid crystal display (LCD) and each line allows up to 16 alphanumeric characters.

Up to 28 alphanumeric and programmable function keys.

Up to 112 kilobytes of memory for application program(s), database, and data entry storage.

EXHIBIT 11.1 Hand-held computer

Courtesy of MSI Data Corporation

EXHIBIT 11.2 Direct connect

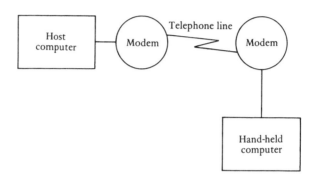

Real-time clock that measures and indicates the time the data was keyed-in.

Power source comes from four alkaline batteries. Two watch cell batteries are used as backup to the main power supply.

Case is lightweight and durable. A see-through plastic keyboard cover can be used for keying-in data in a wet work environment. Also, a carrying case can be purchased to house the hand-held computer.

Has two ways of entering data: via the keyboard or the lightpen for reading zebra-like bar codes.

A small printer can be attached to give a listing of the stored data to meet company, government, and auditing requirements.

Editing can include checking for numeric fields, alpha fields, alphanumeric fields, accumulators, digit validation, inter-record and intra-record relationships.

The programming language is called PROMPT which is similar to RPG II. MSI will do the programming on their equipment or the user can do the programming on the APPLE II personal computer and download the program to the hand-held computer by the use of a program load module. A program load module can have more than one application program and different program load modules can be attached (one at a time) to the hand-held computer and read into storage. Using the program load module approach makes it easier to make programming changes and to reload the program into each hand-held computer.

A communication module can be attached to transmit data to the central computer. Also, data can be transmitted from the central computer to the hand-held computer (i.e., updating table for edit checking).

Excellent field service organization throughout U.S.A., Canada, and Europe.

Depending on memory size and quantity ordered (i.e., discounts), a portable hand-held terminal will cost between $1,000–1,500.

The following are some of the portable terminal applications that can be used:

Electronic ordering

Salesman order entry and retail reporting

Tracking and reporting merchandise movement
Financial reporting
Route sales accounting
Attendance reporting
Direct store delivery
Service reporting
Meter reading
Freight trucking
Maintenance instructions
Quality control
Gathering and tracking data for medical patients
Oil production reporting
Refinery meter reading
Drilling reports
Oil field maintenance reporting
Hydrocarbons emission reporting
Corrosion surveying

In summary, the only limitations in finding applications for the hand-held computer is a person's imagination. They offer potential for source data entry in the field which can mean a 30–60% reduction in data collection *time* and *cost*. All this will mean a large increase in productivity.

12

The
Integrated Electronic
Office

We have traditionally looked first at the application the user needs and then backed into the hardware/software required to meet user requirements. Let us now take the reverse approach and look only at the hardware/software that is multifunctional and flexible.

We shall look at the integrated electronic office of the future which is available now. This super turnkey system combines data processing functions with the electronic counterpart of the typewriter, mail room, and filing cabinet. The name of the company that sells this system will be called Startpoint. Startpoint's system is comprised of the following functions: data processing, word processing, electronic mailbox, and communications management.

Data Processing

Distributed data processing is called to its highest level with Startpoint's EXPAND system. EXPAND has the following advantages:

It provides a computing network which can grow to almost any size or configuration.

Each user has easy access to all of the systems's resources which are user defined. The resources include print spoolers, communication links, and a common database, regardless of location.

It is easy to reconfigure the system. Processors and peripherals can be added, deleted, moved, or functionally altered without disrupting the rest of the system.

The same equipment can be utilized for word processing, electronics mailbox, and communications management.

EXPAND has the following components and facilities:

The three types of functional processors are used for applications, files, and communications. The processors are intelligent video-display keyboard terminals that are easy to use. Also, the system and user memory of each processor can be easily upgraded.

The communications processor is essentially a controller used for polling or addressing the line discipline for external communications.

Processors within one EXPAND system can participate with processors in other EXPAND systems.

The interprocessor bus attaches the processors together, which makes high-speed data exchange possible, and addresses each processor within EXPAND.

The direct channel interface allows a mainframe computer to participate with an application processor in an EXPAND system.

The three types of peripherals used are work station, disk storage, and printer. The work stations are attached to the application processors.

A work station is a low-cost video-display keyboard terminal. The work stations enable a business to share the resources of a single application processor economically. Each application processor can have up to 24 local or remote work stations so that users can enter data, execute programs, communicate, and perform a wide range of other tasks.

The three types of keyboards available for the terminals are standard, data entry, and multifunctional.

EXPAND has its own application development software called TOOLBOX. TOOLBOX uses Startpoint's programming language called TOOLBUS for application development. TOOLBOX will simplify system design, increase programmer productivity, simplify operator training/maintenance, and reduce program development and system life-cycle costs. The TOOLBOX package includes skeleton programs, a data dictionary, generators, and a subroutine library.

The five programming languages available are BASIC, COBOL, FORTRAN, RPG, and TOOLBUS.

See Exhibit 12.1 for a possible EXPAND configuration.

EXHIBIT 12.1 Possible EXPAND configuration

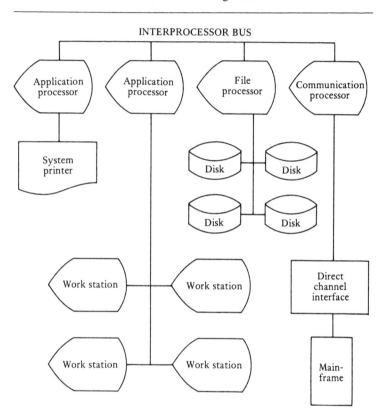

Word Processing

Word processing is just an extension of data processing. The word processing files cohabit with files for data processing and with files for communications management. Having those multiple files available at one location is a unique advantage.

A single work station can generate a letter discussing accounts receivable performance for 10 regions and dig into the database to get numbers for the letter or an attached report. Then instead of typing identical reports and cover letters for 10 regional managers, the terminal can send them out electronically over telephone lines to printers or terminals in the branch offices. By having word processing on the same disk (memory) as communications management, we can queue a word processing message into the telephone system right along with voice messages.

Document management is composed of maintenance and retrieval commands. The following are the commands:

CREATE—	edit a new document
MODIFY—	edit previously created document
ADD—	copy data processing document or file into word processing library
DELETE—	remove document from document library
EXTRACT—	copy document from document library into data processing environment
PACKUP—	reorganize a document library to speed access and save space

DOS—   return to disk operating system (data
                 processing)

The document search and scan facility is made up of inspection and location commands. The following are the commands:

CATALOG—   display names of all documents in
           document library

LOCATE—   display names of documents in which a
           specific text segment occurs

SEARCH—   display any occurrence of a specific segment of text

The six edit keys on the key board are insert/delete, return, backspace, shift, tab, and command.

Word processing's user-controlled format elements are as follows:

Page justification

Even, right, left, or center

Screen displays actual justification

Line spacing

Tab settings

Page headers

Page footers

Page numbering

Margins

Top, bottom, left, or right

Since word processing has straightforward commands, one can:

Skip lines

Delete blocks of text

Boldface and insert left margin

Underline

Move text

Subscript

Insert one document into another

Superscript

Locate a word

Jump to a new page or phrase

Prompt the printer operator

Save blocks of text

Look at embedded format structure

Equate one key to a frequently used phrase or function

Insert blocks of text

Scroll columns up and down from beginning to end and back

Scroll columns from left to right from beginning to end and back

Printing is on high-speed printers and word processing letter-quality printers. Specific pages or the whole document may be printed or spooled for later printing.

Electronic Mailbox

The electronic mailbox is just an extension of the word processing system and communications management which provides easy entry of message information as well as interactive reviewing and filing of electronic messages. This is a vehicle for high-speed message pickup, routing, and delivery.

The electronic mailbox has the following advantages:

It is a timely and cost-effective communication system to make sure that the necessary information is being directed and moved to those who need it in an efficient and controlled manner.

It will reduce the need for separate facilities such as mail rooms, copiers, and communications systems.

It will eliminate duplication of tasks such as retyping or addressing multiple envelopes, thereby increasing office productivity.

The system decides the best manner of distribution and ensures that proper priorities are employed.

The system has been designed to build upon existing equipment with minimum cost and effort.

The company can set the priorities for each message based upon importance and cost. The four priorities are:

OVERNIGHT— message will be delivered and waiting for the recipient first thing in the morning

REGULAR— majority of messages that will have same-day delivery

URGENT— "urgent" messages are routed ahead of the "regular" messages for the same-day delivery

IMMEDIATE— crisis message will go the moment it enters the system and be delivered in a few seconds

For confidential correspondence, the system offers encryption which the sender orders by using a special code. The content of the message is scrambled while the message is in transit. The message will be decrypted if the recipient's definition file includes the special code used by the originator. Also, the system allows further security with verification of delivery and acknowledgment of receipt features.

Management and accounting information is available on a schedule or on-request basis. The reports include information about the system's performance with charge-backs by user, terminal, and/or department. Summary reports are also provided.

Communications Management

Communications management gives the user the tools needed to make trade-offs in telecommunications in terms of cost and service that other business areas have long possessed. These turnkey systems offer the attributes of being easy to install and simple to use.

Four communication systems are available. One, a long distance control system that reduces long distance costs an average of 15–40% through a combination of least-cost routing, queuing, and call buffering. Management and accounting information is available on a scheduled or on-request basis. The reports include detailed and summary information of on-line utilization on every call placed within the corporation by individuals, department, and/or division. The electronic mailbox has the ability to work in conjunction with the long distance control system to transmit messages when there are no voice messages queued and during nonpeak calling hours. The long distance control system acts as a traffic manager by interleaving message traffic into the valleys between peak telephone traffic usage. Essentially, the message is given a free ride, since the user is already paying for unused flat-rate capacity. See Exhibit 12.2 for an overview of message and voice traffic usage.

Two, a short distance control system that is an extended application of the long distance control system for monitoring local and toll charge calls. This system helps communications management to allocate costs accurately, adjust facilities, and optimize service for local calling.

Three, a multilocation control system that is a combination of the long/short distance control systems for a multilocation company that needs a simple means of centralizing its communications. The multilocations take care of the details of actual call placement, but communications management and reporting occurs at the user's headquarters.

Four, an incoming-calls control system provides efficient processing of high-volume incoming telephone calls and makes optimum use of existing telephone facilities. Flexibility in call processing and queuing allows a company to operate more efficiently and economically while providing better service.

EXHIBIT 12.2 Message and voice traffic usage

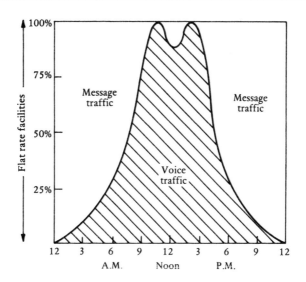

Conclusions

The integrated electronic office of the future moves computer technology into the office now with systems that look to the future as they meet current needs. The integrated approach means having a family of systems using general-purpose processors that can do a variety of jobs. As you can see, the end is just beginning.

13

Our
Computer-Based
Society

Everyones's life is affected in some shape or form by the microcomputer and its changing technology. We are constantly finding more uses for the microcomputer (especially at home) which will have an increasing effect in changing our lives in the 1980s. Our computer-based society will have a growing, profound impact on our financial, social, and political machinery. The speed of change could have a multiplier affect on our lives which will be especially strong from 1985–1990 and then leveling off at a slower rate of change. Because of microcomputer technology, the author sees the following high visibility areas starting to change or affect our lives.

Electronics Funds Transfer (EFT)

PAST AND CURRENT PROBLEMS IN EFT GROWTH

Privacy—principal privacy concerns are related to disclosure of personal data in EFT systems by government or private surveillance.

Security—vulnerabilities such as a high number of access points, difficulty of crime detections, and a reduction in the effectiveness or elimination of some traditional means of control and auditing.

Equity—could displace, reduce, or raise the costs of alternatives which means some subgroups could experience a loss of equity.

Human behavior—against change towards new technology.

NETWORKS IN PLACE

VISA

Mastercard (master teller)

ADP (the exchange)

American Express (ready cash)

Sears and Roebuck

Fed and Bank Wire

Merrill, Lynch, Pierce, Fenner & Smith

Automated Teller Machine (ATM) networks

Clearing House Interbank Payments System (CHIPS)

Society for Worldwide Interbank Financial Telecommunications (SWIFT)

TRENDS

1. New laws will be enacted to protect privacy and security. Also, new control features/devices will be built into EFT networks. Therefore, people will find EFT to be more convenient, reliable, and safe to use.

2. More people will be working at home and "telecommuting" by using a computer terminal. The number of personal computers being sold for the home is doubling every year and it is expected that three million will be sold in 1983. In truth, you can always do better when you're selling a new product in an unsaturated market. All this means is that people will be more inclined to stay home and pay their bills electronically.

3. A system that will link home televisions with computerized data banks will allow us to pay bills electronically.

4. Credit cards will get a lot smarter and could be called "chip cards." Cards would have integrated circuit chips (replacing the magnetic strip) imbedded in them for storing information so that the card could be updated each time it is used to keep track of all banking and retail transactions.

CONCLUSIONS

The global market for information handling and telecommunications will soar. For example, American Bell, the subsidiary of AT&T, will offer a service that allows unrelated computer systems to communicate with one another across the country.

EFT tends to receive more publicity in retail areas such as ATM and point-of-sale terminals than it does in corporate applications. However, it is in the corporate sector (including government agency and corporate accounts) that EFT will have the greatest impact. The fast growth of EFT will finally eliminate float. The author predicts that by January 1, 1990, there will be no float within or between the United States and Europe. Corporations and banks will be better able to quantify their rates of return on investments and their cost of capital as they become better informed of their funds position. In summary, we are becoming a cashless society.

CORPORATIONS:
Information Factories

The parameters of the factory and the production line will be used by corporations to establish for white collar workers the criteria of productivity for the "information factory." In other words, they are looking at the individual's output and ways to increase it on the assumption that if tasks can be completed sooner the corporation's productivity will show a related increase.

In order to improve the productivity of people, behavioral changes are needed, changes in the way people think about and handle their jobs. Such changes take time and the productivity gains occur gradually. Technological changes affect us physically. Efforts to reduce their harmful effects by controlling the environment show our awareness of this problem. But the new technologies also create severe emotional, situational, and social changes whose effect is less easy to notice or modify. Patterns of thought and sequences of actions, based on earlier assumptions are—to an increasingly greater degree—becoming unreliable in their ability to help us prepare for a future that is upon us almost in the instant we know enough to predict it.

For productivity to improve at all levels within the "information factory," it will be necessary for all of us to learn how to revise our ways of seeing and doing things, so that we may be able to combine complex new technologies into synergistic concepts. Corporations will train their people for the new systems. The new systems should be well-defined, allow time for a reasonable learning curve, and be user-friendly. Because of the new technologies, corporations will orient their operating budgets to the future, not the past—base them on future needs, not on past actuals.

TRENDS

Small business and even individual departments within large corporations are turning to microcomputers to boost productivity and save money.

Corporations will have to control the proliferations of microcomputers, especially the ones that share common files.

Quality circles will be used as the key to employee involvement in improving productivity.

More ergonomics—the matching of machine design to human comfort.

Use of display phones—speaker, automatic redial, pre-dialing, recall listing, calendar reminders, and automatic log-on to external data processing systems (e.g., Dow Jones).

Use of voice technology—voice recognition, voice storage, and voice retrieval equipment.

More teleconferencing networks.

More global communications (e.g., satellites).

Electronic magazines, newspapers, and mail.

Use of touch-sensor screens for input versus keyboards for some applications.

More sophisticated graphics.

Use of thinking (artificial intelligence) computers.

Management, salespeople, and data processing auditors using portable personal computers that are briefcase-sized work stations.

Use of more robots on the assembly lines.

Corporations will try more application software (e.g., electronic worksheets).

Corporations will try more user-friendly programming languages for nonprogrammers to learn and use.

Corporate data processing departments will do more "marketing" to their end users to educate them and make them more aware of available data processing services.

Home TV Trends

With compatible terminal and telephone lines the following trends will appear:

More working at home (telecommute to work).

Electronic newspapers, magazines, and mail.

Business and economic news from major financial centers.

Transfer bank funds and pay for purchases remotely.

Security—24-hour-a-day protection for home and family against burglaries, fires, and common household emergencies.

Home climate controllers.

More cable programs.

Use of holograms (a 3-D image produced with lasers).

General applications—programming, entertainment, education, hobbies.

Specific applications—budgeting, word processing, mailing lists, calendar reminders, recipes, computing income tax, track and control household expenses, inventory possessions, database management.

Looking up doctors, plumbers, and other service people.

Voting will eventually be possible.

Revolution in Education

Personal computers will be used in elementary and high schools; they will be mandatory for all college and university students at a relatively low cost with high resale value. Students will be able to use the microcomputer for normal class assignments and special programs. Computer camps, clubs, and playparks will help children prepare themselves for careers in a computer-based society.

Electronic Warfare Systems

Hookups between computers in the cockpits of planes and battlefield command centers will give pilots a complete picture of ground and air threats beyond the horizon in a 100-mile radius. The computers will also rank the targets in the order of their importance and assign attack priorities.

Computers will be used to simulate war games.

Computers will be used to blind energy radars and eavesdrop on enemy battlefield communications.

Computers will be used to disrupt the ability of enemy commanders to talk with their troops while keeping its own radio-communications resistant to jamming.

Other

Medical science will use more computerized microcircuits for artificial limbs and organs. Motor vehicles will use microcomputers for navigation aids, greater fuel economy, and control of engine transmissions.

Conclusions

Prior to the 1980s approximately 70% of hardware/software expenditures were paid for by the data processing departments for their usage (e.g., giving service to the end-users). In the mid-1980s this trend will reverse and the end-users will be making approximately 70% of the data processing expenditures for their own usage (e.g., hardware/software for the office and the plant floor). This is an indication that the minicomputer market will grow approximately three times faster than the large computer market.

We are going to have to retrain people who lose their jobs for the computer-based society. The United States Government should take a leadership role in the direction of retraining people. More and more, workers will shift to service jobs and fast-growing, high-technology industries—aerospace, telephones, computers, and home electronics. For some the transition will hurt. But an older, better-trained work force plus gains in automation will mean higher productivity.

The computer-based society will modify old social issues and create new ones. But the pluses of the microcomputers, large computers, and supercomputers will far outweigh the minuses (e.g., computer crime is on the increase) of change. Finally, the only limitations we will have with computers will be our imaginations.

Glossary

Access method. The manner (random or sequential) in which records are added to or retrieved from peripheral storage.

ANSI (American National Standards Institute). An international organization that devised a group of standardized symbols used in flow charting.

ASCII (American Standard Code for Information Interchange). A computer code used with terminal devices.

Assembler language. A source language that translates single commands into single machine-code instructions to the computer.

BASIC (Beginners All-purpose Symbolic Instruction Code). An easy to learn, high-level, algebra-like language designed for use in problem solving.

Batch processing. A system that accumulates the transactions for an application over a period of time and then processes all of them as a group.

Binary. A numbering system that consists of two distinct characters, 0 or 1.

195

Bits (BInary digiTS). Either a 0 or a 1 state.

Buffer. A temporary storage device attached to the CPU and used for transmitting data from one device to another.

Byte. Commonly represents eight bits which equals one byte or one character.

Chip. Miniaturized integrated circuit made from silicon.

COBOL (COmmon Business Oriented Language). A high-level language used primarily in business applications.

COM (Computer Output Microfilm). A method of storing large amounts of data on microfilm through a COM printer.

Compiler. A translating program that converts a high-level source-language program into a machine-language program.

CPU (Central Processing Unit). A unit of a computer that controls the interpretation and execution of instructions.

CRT (Cathode Ray Tube). A visual display terminal that uses a TV picture tube.

Database. A general term for a collection of related data files used by a computer system.

Data communications. The transmission and reception of data.

Data processing department. A group (e.g., operations, programming, and systems) that provides data processing (DP) services within a company or an outside organization.

DDP (Distributed Data Processing). Having computer processing power and databases at remote locations.

Diskette. A thin, flexible magnetic disk and a semi-rigid protective jacket used with minicomputer systems to provide disk storage capacity.

Disk storage. Storage on direct access devices that record data magnetically on the flat surfaces of one or more disks that rotate in use.

EBCDIC (Extended Binary Coded Decimal Interchange Code). A byte or character used to represent data stored in a computer.

Firmware. Software that is incorporated on a chip.

FORTRAN (FORmula TRANslation). A high-level, algebra-like language designed for use in scientific applications.

Hardcopy. A printed copy of machine output (e.g., report).

Hardware. Physical equipment found in a computer system.

JCL (Job Control Language). Statements in a job that are used to identify the job or describe its requirements to the system.

Mass storage. A device having a large storage capacity that is accessible to a computer.

Memory. A general term for auxiliary or main storage of data that is accessible to the processor.

Minicomputer. A physically small and relatively inexpensive computer that possesses the potential of a larger computer but to a limited degree.

MODEM (MOdulator-DEModulator). A device that modulates and demodulates signals transmitted over data communication facilities.

Multiprocessing. Parallel processing of two or more computer programs or sequences of instructions by a computer or computer network.

Multiprogramming. Parallel execution of two or more programs by a computer.

Object program. An output program from a compiler that is in machine-readable form.

Off-line. Devices that are not under the control of the CPU.

On-line. Devices that are under the control of the CPU.

PL/1. A high-level programming language designed for use in a wide range of commercial and scientific computer applications.

Program. Routines or detailed instructions for the computer to perform.

Program flow chart. A pictorial representation of the machine functions within a computer program.

RAM (Random Access Memory). Working storage of minicomputer in which data can be stored and accessed.

Real time processing. A computer system that processes transactions as they occur.

ROM (Read Only Memory). Software that is incorporated on a chip by which data or instructions are read only.

RPG (Report Program Generator). A programming language designed to facilitate the output of business reports.

Software. All programs and operating instructions that are concerned with the operation of a data processing system.

Sort. To segregate items into groups which are specified by a sort key associated with each record.

System flow chart. A general representation of the overall system that indicates interrelationships between the organization and/or computer process.

Time-sharing. An on-line method that allows a number of users to execute programs concurrently in a large computer system.

Update. An operation that can add, change, or delete records in a file.

Utility. A computer program written to solve common (e.g., sorts and merges) problems encountered by programmers or users.

Bibliography

DeMarco, T. *Structured Analysis and System Specifications.* New York: Yourdon Inc., 1978.

Griffin, Robert C. "Relational Diagramming." *Data Management*, March 1978, p. 48–53.

HIPO—A Design Aid and Documentation Technique. IBM Publication GC20-1851.

Katzan, Harry, Jr. *Distributed Data Processing.* New York: Petrocelli Books, 1978.

Martin, James. *Application Development without Programmers.* Englewood Cliffs, N.J.: Prentice-Hall, 1982.

Orilia, Lawrence S. *Introduction to Business Data Processing.* New York: McGraw-Hill, 1979.

Ramsgard, William C. *Making Systems Work.* New York: John Wiley & Sons, 1977.

———. "The Systems Analyst: Doctor of Business." *Journal of Systems Management*, July 1974, p. 18–23.

Smith, Ronald B. "FLOPS Flops . . . But Why?" *Data Management*, July 1979, p. 26–28.

____. *How to Plan, Design and Implement a Bad System.* New York: Petrocelli Books, 1981.

____. "Model for Documenting Controls Strengthens Weak Auditing Link." *Data Management*, May 1977, p. 18–22.

Swann, Gloria Harrington. *Top-Down Structured Design Techniques.* New York: Petrocelli Books, 1978.

Warnier, Jean-Dominique. *Logical Construction of Systems.* New York: Van Nostrand Reinhold, 1982.

Yourdon, Edward and Constantine, Larry L. *Structured Design.* Englewood Cliffs, N.J.: Prentice-Hall, 1979.

Index